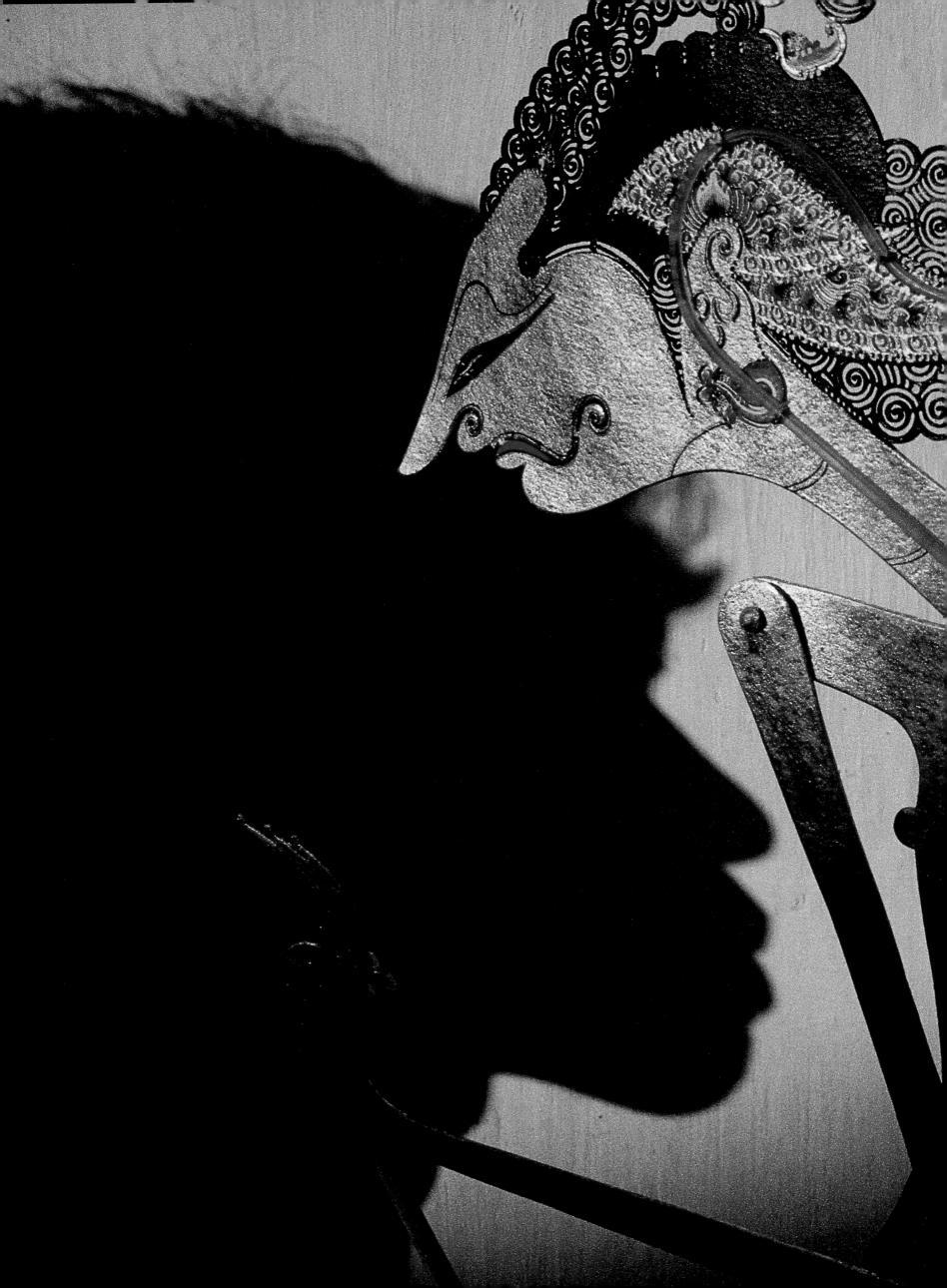

EDITORIAL ADVISORY BOARD

Ali Alatas, Minister of Foreign Affairs, Republic of Indonesia
Hariati Sœbadio, Minister for Social Welfare, Republic of Indonesia
Sabam Siagian, Editor, the *Jakarta Post*

PUBLISHERS

Joop Ave
Didier Millet
Kevin Weldon
John Owen

PROJECT DIRECTOR

Dawn Low

PROJECT EDITOR

Peter Schoppert

PHOTOGRAPHY

Chief Photographer Rio Helmi
Assignment Coordinator Anna S. Kusumo
Advisor R.M. Soelaeman Pringgodigdo, Department of Foreign Affairs
Research Etnodata

PROJECT COORDINATORS

Editorial Gillian Young
Sponsorship Ibu Seti-Arti Kailola
Public Relations Halida Ilahunde-Leclerc
Travel and Logistics Anne Greensall
Logistics and Government Liaison (Dirgen Pariwisata)
Peter Pangaribuan, Juniarti, Asahari Abdullah, Tjetjep Suparman
Jakarta Hilton Rudy Salleh
French Edition Françoise Job
Italian Edition Corinne Hewlett

CREATIVE DIRECTOR

Leonard Lueras

DESIGN

Patrick Lébedeff
Archival Research Leo Haks
Picture Selection Marie-Claude Millet, Carolyn Watts, Annette Crueger
Layout Louise Brody, Jean-Noël Doan, Chan Mei Ling

PRODUCTION

Philippe Marchand and Jimmy Kang

PROJECT ACCOUNTANT

Drs Siddharta & Siddharta in association with
Coopers & Lybrand,
with Christian Tenggono, Cathy Chacko and Nicholas Bale

A VOYAGE THROUGH THE ARCHIPELAGO

BY 45 OF THE WORLD'S

LEADING PHOTOGRAPHERS

AUGUST THE 26TH

TO SEPTEMBER THE 4TH 1989

NESIA

IN COMMEMORATION

OF THE 45TH ANNIVERSARY

OF THE PROCLAMATION

OF INDEPENDENCE

FOREWORD BY GAVIN YOUNG

TEXT BY EDWARD BEHR

CAPTIONS BY PAUL ZACH

ARCHIPELAGO PRESS

Sails in the Sulawesi Straits *(this page and preceding)*. Views from the deck of a Bugis schooner somewhere between Java and Sulawesi are almost surreal: fishermen still maneuver their traditional low-slung *prahu* across the glossy waters with upturned sails aerodynamically-designed for Indonesia's often breathless airs.
Bernard Hermann, *France*

(pages 10/11) The *merah putih*, Indonesia's red and white flag, anchors a *kora kora* canoe full of Bandanese paddling furiously past Gunung Api volcano. Canoe races are regularly held in the lagoon off the coast of Banda Neira, the tiny capital town of the Banda islands.
Wendy Chan, *Singapore*

(pages 12/13) Unlike seas in the northern Pacific where marine life has been devastated by drift-netting, traditional fishing techniques prevail in most of the archipelago. And scenes like this one off the coast of Seram are still common.
Rio Helmi, *Indonesia*

(pages14/15) Dusk in Central Java. The Javanese farmer, and Indonesians from Sumatra to Irian Jaya, must cope with great changes in their lives: whether it is the allure of big city living, or new ways of farming and working the land.
Gerald Gay, *Singapore*

—— CONTENTS ——

The outrig rises on a crest, then dips through the green water rushing past. The bow-wave hisses, the prahu's turquoise sail cracks in the varying wind, and I see an expanse of sea glittering like shot-silk, the low black contour of a distant coastline and a long white beach, and a great rampart of mountain half lost in rising wisps of cloud, as if the jungle floor was on fire. This is how I see Indonesia in my mind's eye: from the deck of a boat. I have been lucky in this respect. At intervals over the last twenty-five years, I have spent months mooning about the seemingly boundless waters that separate the Bay of Bengal from every sea and strait from Aceh to Aru, waters that unite as well as divide the islands that lie like slumbering green sea monsters under the passionate sun. I can never be tired of them or of the soft-eyed, friendly people who inhabit them.

Sometimes I have seen them from the wooden deck of a prahu; once from an old ketch built in Dorset, England, in 1912; sometimes cocooned in the air-conditioned luxury of a PELNI steamer, the Indonesian Government Line. (The smaller the vessel the better, to be as close as possible to the elements.) Ideally, islands of such beauty, such works of natural art, should be approached slowly and circumspectly — to avoid bumping into the ubiquitous reefs, of course, but also to give the local magic time to work. The mood of any particular coastline reveals itself in its own good time.

Adventurous men have been negotiating these islands for thousands of years. Sailors all, Magellan, Francis Drake and Joseph Conrad are among them. Here, more than anywhere else in Southeast Asia, you are in a world of seafarers. The Buginese and Mandarese people — the 'orang pelaut' of Sulawesi (Celebes in the old world), and colonizers par excellence of the region from Selangor and Malacca in what is now Malaysia to Kutei and Bau-bau — are among the world's greatest sailors and boat-builders. Most Indonesians still choose to visit other islands by boat rather than by plane. Why not us?

In my recent voyages in Southeast Asia I have been rediscovering the world of Joseph Conrad. The search for traces of the world he knew as a ship's captain has taken me around a good many islands, up several remote rivers and across quite a few bumpy mountain roads. I have been living a good deal with the ghosts of the people he encountered (and later wrote about) in South Sulawesi, the northeast of Kalimantan, southern Sumatra and East Java. They are the phantoms of several races, colors and religions, including Buginese, Malays, Arabs, British and Dutch. Furthermore, I began my search from Conrad's exact starting point off southeast Sumatra, moving up the Bangka Strait towards Muntok on the bridge of a steamer. There I had better luck than he: His ship was carrying a cargo of coal from England to Bangkok when it caught fire off Java Head and officers and crew were *obliged to take to the boats. As a young officer, Conrad was in charge of one of these, from which he had his first vision of the East. When I sailed the Bangka Strait aboard the PELNI ship Lawit, I held in front of me the pages of Conrad's 'Youth' in which he described the scene as it appeared a hundred years ago.*

What I actually saw made rather a gloomy scene. The coast of Sumatra lay close on our port side, but barely visible in a heavy storm cloud. To the east, rain fell over Bangka Island, over its hilly skyline from which giant tree-tops thrust up like the dripping crests of long-necked exotic birds. Of this place Conrad wrote, "I remember the heat, the deluge of rain squalls that kept us bailing for dear life (but filled our water-cask), and I remember sixteen hours on end with a mouth dry as a cinder and a steering-oar over the stern to keep my first command head-on to a breaking sea." Conrad and his fellow survivors of the shipwreck arrived at the little port of Muntok utterly exhausted. I too presently arrived there, although, I need hardly say, with little effort on my part. We were both in our own way exhilarated by what we saw.

You do not have to be shipwrecked to share such exhilaration on first sight of Indonesia, but it certainly helps to be seabound. Conrad goes on, "Now I see a high outline of mountains … a wide bay as smooth as glass … And suddenly a puff of wind, a puff faint and tepid and laden with strange odors of blossoms, of aromatic wood, comes out of the still night — the first sigh of the East on my face."

I have felt that first sigh. Of course, it is not essential to go to the Bangka Strait to feel it, but even the most romantically inclined are unlikely to feel it from the seat of a plane.

Of all my early seaborne impressions, I remember best my first sight of Macassar (the colonial name for the port that is now officially Ujung Pandang). Its mosques, its churches with their steeples like witches' hats, are at their greatest from a certain distance, framed by a bodyguard of tree-topped reefs and patrolled by clusters of little sailing vessels flitting like moths in the sunlight. The Dutch fort is barely visible, but the low line of this historic trading port spreads itself dramatically against the background of fortress mountains that seem to line up as guards to the ancient Buginese kingdoms of Wajo and Bone, like some forbidding fairy-tale escarpment. There, in olden days, battles raged as constantly as the rajahs' alliances shifted. Listen carefully and you may even fancy you can hear the clash of swords and krisses, the roar of old Dutch or Portuguese cannon. Is it merely thunder?

The approach to Bali, either from Lombok or from the direction of Surabaya or Banyuwangi, is hard to beat. Possibly only the approach by sea to Ternate from Ambon can truly rival it: that incredible procession of volcanoes placed like milestones in the Moluccan Sea, a giant causeway to clove-bearing Halmahera, and then on to Irian Jaya where the elusive Birds of Paradise lurk in forest glades as silent as temples.

You meet so many changes of mood in the Indonesian landscape, not all of them as obviously attractive as those of Bali or Tanah Toraja. I speak for myself in confessing, for example, to a great affection for the hidden rivers of East Kalimantan. They can appear somber. They are Conradian even now, almost untouched, although for how much longer, given the world's insatiable hunger for timber and oil? Somber, yes, but romantic too. The central character of 'Lord Jim', Conrad's best-known novel, met his end up one of these rivers, and the characters of Almayer and Captain Lingard in Conrad's first book, 'Almayer's Folly', were based on real people river-trading in these parts. Arabs from Singapore also sailed trading ships up these 'lost' streams. Some of them made their fortunes and stayed, and their descendants are there to this day, as Indonesian citizens now, of course, living side-by-side with the Dayaks.

I am not particularly brave, but I am quite happy to find myself in a small boat in some remote corner of the Straits of Macassar. It is no matter if it rains, the seas are lumpy and big, and the waves fill the foredeck with green water. As far as I am concerned, the romance of the place takes over. One is alone with nature then, and no doubt a few friendly dolphins.

Once, in an old ketch, my friends and I had a friendly race with a Buginese prahu for a mile or two off the coast of Kalimantan. It was a fine, thoroughbred boat, but we won the race. Then we moored side-by-side for the best part of a day and made friends with the crew. Three months later we met again by chance in the little Sulawesi post of Dongala. This time, the prahu's crew buckled to uninvited and built us a dugout canoe with an outrig. It was an extraordinary and touching act of friendship. The last time I had seen them they were flying up the Straits of Macassar, their great striped mainsail billowing beautifully and the spray spouting up from their bows. A hundred years ago, in headbands and sarongs, they might have been taken for pirates. I heard a terrific shout and, thrilled by the echo of my name across that romantic sheet of water, I looked to see their white teeth and frantic waving. We all waved until we could see each other no more.

Other times, other images. I remember being on a small boat turning into a silent river-mouth where the water is phosphorescent and there is no one left in the world except perhaps for a fisherman in a small dugout under the mangroves. The rain falls in collonades; the nipa palms lisp and rattle along the riverbank. But the storm soon passes, the sky clears, in a blaze of flame the sun sets. After dark, night birds whoosh overhead against a moon that silvers the muddy water. You slap at the mosquitoes, occasional fires glow on the bank, someone laughs in a tiny stilted house - and you are at the beginning of the world. Sometimes I would like my own small stilted house at the beginning of this world.

Perhaps that is too melancholy a scene for some people. For them there is a lighter magic elsewhere, a magic I believe to be just as real. It creeps into your ears in the music of Java, in the sweet, dream-like sounds of the gamelan that are often, and accurately, described as liquid moonlight. It would be magical to live on Java Head looking out over the Sunda Strait at the black, soaring, darkly sinister shape of the most famous of eastern volcanoes, Krakatau. How wonderful it would be to watch - from a safe distance - it vomiting its cataracts of lava. Further up the coast of Sumatra you can wander about the white moonlit ramparts and cloisters of Fort Marlborough at Bengkulu (Bencoolen to the British) where Raffles governed briefly after founding Singapore, and where there is a small but interesting old British cemetery. There are all sorts of colourful ghosts of the past in Indonesia and all, as far as I know, are amiable. They are almost as much a part of the scene as the living. Leaving aside Borobudur and Java's many other ancient temples, there is a finely restored cemetery in Jakarta, an unrestored one in Surabaya, another in Macassar, and there are no doubt others elsewhere. There is history for everyone in Indonesia. Above all, so little has changed since Conrad and the Buginese sea rovers sailed these waters. A hundred years ago they saw more or less what we see now under an identical equatorial sun. You cannot say that about many countries in the world, not by a very long chalk. Here in the enchanted islands of the Archipelago, made famous in the West by Alfred Russell Wallace and so many other literary travellers, we can still experience Indonesia as Conrad did. We can still gaze at those high outlines of mountains, blue in the morning, jagged walls of purple at sunset, and those wide bays, 'smooth as glass and polished like ice'; we can feel the same soft, warm night, and the puff of wind laden with odours of blossoms and aromatic wood - the sigh of the East on our faces. Like Conrad, we can leave Indonesia at last and never again forget its charm, 'impalpable and enslaving, like a whispered promise of mysterious delight.' And if by some improbable chance the images of these enchanted islands do begin to fade, we can always open this book to refresh our memories and renew our delight.

Indonesia's exotic cultures and landscapes have attracted writers and artists from the West at least since the Portuguese arrived in the 16th century. They brought back vivid descriptions and drawings that spawned romantic notions about the islands. Then photographers arrived almost as soon as the camera was invented early in the 19th century – and the images they recorded confirmed those notions *(preceding)*.

E arly photographers bravely lugged their bulky plate cameras to the farthest corners of the archipelago, although the steam railroad systems built by the Dutch in Java and Sumatra *(top left)* made the going easier. These scenes of misty Mount Sumbing *(bottom left)*, smoking Mount Bromo *(top right)* and rice paddy fields near Yogyakarta *(bottom right)* were photo-graphed by O. Kurkdjian around 1920.

Indonesia's rich agricultural potential was tapped by the Dutch: plantations were especially successful in the late 19th century, growing tobacco (top), coffee, sugar, rubber and tea. But for most of the country, the village remained the basic agricultural unit, like this hamlet in the highlands of Sumatra *(bottom)*.

While there have been Indonesian cities for thousands of years, they did not always conform to the European idea of what a city should look like. So the Dutch built their colonial capitals in their own image, with boulevards and canals. The morning rush hour in Jakarta, then still known as Batavia, was somewhat less hectic in 1940 *(top)* – and the main street in Medan saw only the occasional breakdown of a water buffalo in 1898 *(bottom)*.

They were usually not participants, but early photographers were interested in the daily goings-on in Indonesian village life, and they knew that 'quaint' scenes like these would appeal to big city dwellers and to colonials who bought photograph albums. There was a great demand for staged shots which attempted to convey a sense of typical Indonesian daily life, like these men playing cards *(top)*, a snack-time scene *(top right)* and the hunting scene complete with wild boar *(below)*.

Cock-fighting *(bottom)* was and is a Balinese pastime which attracts a great deal of attention. The Balinese had an exceedingly complex unwritten system of betting, nearly impossible for an outsider to follow, which – so say the anthropologists – reflected the intricate web of social obligation and interaction that is Balinese society. While gambling on these rooster rousts is officially not allowed, cockfights are permitted on Bali for religious and ritual purposes.

The pageantry and theatre of the Javanese courts were a popular subject for early photographers in Indonesia. The sultans too understood the appeal of photographs, and in the late 19th century patronage by the courts was as sought after by photographers as it was by artists and craftsmen working in the more traditional arts of Java. And these traditional arts were one of the more popular subjects of early photographers. The costumes of the Solo court are captured *(top)*, as well as the instruments of a small gamelan ensemble *(bottom)*.

Despite their long history and remarkable continuity, dance and drama in Indonesia are not static, stiff and unchanging *(top)*. Improvisation and individual innovations are often welcomed, as are foreign influences. The *kecak* dance *(bottom)* which seems to foreigners so quintessentially Balinese was in fact invented in the 1920s, with the collaboration of foreign artists, for a film on Bali.

T he advent of photography meant the advent of the wedding portrait, even in Bali *(left)*. This superb picture of the newlyweds, taken by an unknown photographer around 1910, exhibits remarkable detail. Javanese sultans also posed for posterity, fully decked out with their medals and heirloom *keris* daggers.

Despite the stiff poses, there is genuine charm in vintage portraits of a classical dancer *(top right)* and a haji, a Muslim pilgrim just returned from Mecca *(bottom right)* by Tio Tek Hong, *circa* 1920. The man *(top left)* holding the world's largest flower, the Rafflesia, has a stern expression, and no wonder: the flower gives out an awful carrion stench. The Sumatran scent-maker *(bottom left)* carries his fighting bird in a cage, circa 1905–1925.

The richness and appeal of Indonesian textiles can be seen in this portrait of two Minangkabau women. They wear sarongs of batik, probably of the sort made in Java specifically for the Sumatran market. Their headdresses and shoulder cloths are made of *songket*, a cloth which incorporates gold and silver threads to form a luxurious finish.

Groet uit
Losarang (Indramajoe)

Prampoean pidjit — Masseuse.

Pretty women have always captured the eye – and the camera lenses – of photographers. The special look of Javanese beauties *(right and bottom left)* was no exception. Even the resolute Dutch explorer C Nieuwenhuis could not resist snapping a picture of a Minang-kabau woman in Padang (*bottom right) circa* 1900. And an enterprising photographer named Ali S Cohan came up with the prototype of the cheesy postcard *(top left).*

INDONESIA REVISITED

I was nineteen years old and the Second World War had only just ended. I had no idea that for me another war was about to begin. As a junior officer I had been posted to a battalion of the Indian Army stationed at Padang, West Sumatra, which was part of a brigade whose original task had been to disarm the Imperial Japanese Army in September 1945. It was soon embroiled in a local guerilla war against the Tentara Nasional Indonesia, staging a holding operation on behalf of the Dutch who did not take over the area until November 1946.

This was hardly an auspicious start to a love story, but the truth is I fell in love with Indonesia from the moment I landed in Medan. I was still immature in many ways and the memory of these months has remained with me ever since. I was not the only one for whom the Indonesian archipelago provided a seminal experience: Dirk Bogarde, the distinguished actor turned author, also came to Indonesia in British Army uniform in 1945, and in his novels and moving autobiography wrote extensively about those strange, twilight months when we were neither truly at war nor at peace. For both of us, the experience could well have been brutalizing. It had a contrary effect instead. The unforgettable natural beauty of the land, its cultural and artistic wealth, and the charm of its people had an immediate impact.

I knew I was witnessing at first hand the long overdue demise of a colonial era. My passionate interest in history and world affairs dates from that initial experience. I vowed that I would return, and did so, for *Newsweek* in the sixties. Indonesia underwent enormous changes between 1946 and 1967, but has changed just as much since, and given the chance to contribute to this magnificently illustrated book, I accepted unhesitatingly, though with diffidence: so many people know far more about it than I do.

On my first flight to Sumatra, I had been the only human passenger aboard a DC 3 with a herd of live goats destined for Indian Army kukris. On my most recent visit, aboard a packed, but comfortable Garuda Airlines plane, I felt something of the wonder that comes from time-warped memories of long ago. The faces and the older passengers' clothing had not changed, but the environment was not the same. I remembered wooden and wattle bungalows, and puddles in unpaved streets, but had to take the winding road to Bukittinggi to find their present-day equivalents. Although Padang had become a modern town, however, there was still the magically familiar surrounding landscape of rolling hills, mist-covered mountains and bush-topped trees. Above all, there were the sounds, of heavy rain on green tin roofing, of hymn-singing from a dozen different Christian mission churches. Drenched and mezmerized by the childrens' pure voices, I was rooted to the spot. In 1946 I had often wondered what this infinitely remote, romantic land would come to. Its people seemed secure in their beliefs despite the onslaughts of sudden modernity. In fact, they appeared to have weathered the intervening years better than I.

It is not usually wise to return to the scene of one's first love, for reality cannot compete with idealized memories. This time, however, not only was I not disappointed, but I also fully realized the mythical 'lure of the islands' that so gripped Joseph Conrad and many other great writers. It is this sense of wonder, of excitement, so compellingly rendered by some of the world's greatest photographers, that I have tried to convey. Indonesia is not just a cluster of islands. The scope, variety and sheer dimensions of this nation are more on the scale of a continent and are better related in pictures than in words. Above all, it has to be experienced.

Edward Behr

fifteen million years ago, though many of the islands were still connected even in the most recent Ice Age. The biggest of these, Kalimantan (Borneo), Irian (the Indonesian half is Irian Jaya, the rest Papua New Guinea), Sumatra, Sulawesi (Celebes) and of course Java, are country-sized, and indeed Indonesia itself has a continental rather than national dimension. Sumatra is slightly larger than Sweden, Sulawesi bigger than Great Britain. Though not all its islands or atolls are of volcanic origin, the volcano dominates the Indonesian landscape and its people, physically and spiritually, just as Mount Fuji dominates Japan. Volcanoes are both Indonesia's blessing and its curse, the source of its riches and of its barrenness, almost certainly shaping its peoples' beliefs, myths and migrations as well. The alluvial plains of Java, Bali and certain parts of Sumatra are the by-product of volcanic eruptions. Without them, the land would be less fertile, its ecology vastly different. Since the beginning of recorded time, word-of-mouth history all over the archipelago has told of fire spouting from the mountaintops, deluging the surrounding countryside with molten lava. Some eruptions, of course, predate even 'Java Man' (*pithecanthropus erectus*), the planet's oldest two-legged inhabitant. Our common ancestor — an Indonesian — lived a near-human existence nearly two million years ago.

Practically my first view ever of Indonesia was from the cockpit of a DC 3 flying to Padang, West Sumatra, in 1946. What kind of a country was this, I asked myself, that had a huge lake at the top of what appeared to be a large volcano, and an island in the middle of the lake? This, of course, was Lake Toba, one of the largest, highest, deepest lakes in the world, so large that the island of Samosir in its center covers 1,055 square kilometers. Lake Toba is reckoned to be the outcome of one of the earth's greatest convulsions several million years ago.

Californians pride themselves on their hedonistic fatalism, living as they do over a major fault line that threatens not only their way of life but the entire West Coast economy. But most Indonesians live their whole lives in much closer proximity to

Bawomataluwo, Nias: An *adu zatua* carving in the royal palace concentrates power and forces for fertility in an ancestral figure. **Darwis Triadi,** *Indonesia*

disaster and sudden death. In 1815, the eruption of Mount Tambora on Sumbawa Island (east of Bali and Lombok and bigger than either) projected 100 cubic kilometers of matter into the air, killing 90,000 people and obscuring the sun all over the Indonesian archipelago, causing such a durable atmospheric haze that 1816 has gone down in history as the 'year without a summer'. On a tiny, uninhabited island, Mount Krakatau's eruption in 1883 caused huge tidal waves to sweep inland into Sumatra and West Java, killing 35,000 people. The explosion was heard as far away as western Australia, and became a favorite theme for writers and film-makers. Hardly a month goes by without one of Indonesia's seventy active volcanoes reminding the world at large, gently or otherwise, of their presence. So much so, that quite major eruptions, which in Europe or America would make frontpage news, are not even reported outside Indonesia itself. There the threat is such that government disaster prevention techniques are the most highly developed in the world: farmers living on volcanic slopes anywhere in Indonesia know they will get fair warning of any eruption.

Tilang, Flores: The coconut serves in many roles. The water is refreshing, its pulp delicious, and the husk yields copra and coconut oil.
Michael Freeman, *UK*

Not all volcanic activity has been good for the soil. Even parts of the paradise island of Bali bear witness to that. On its northernmost tip, the foot of Mount Batur is a depressing landscape of black, volcanic stone, and the people living there, toughened and impoverished by their harsh environment, are thought to be unfriendly, predatory, and quick to take offence. They are also, hardly coincidentally, compulsive gamblers.

Dozens of erudite volumes illustrate Indonesia's flora and fauna, and yet they remain relatively undiscovered country. Books about the Sumatran rainforest alone, with its intricate, inter-related jumble of life-supporting vegetation, would fill several library shelves. It was Sir Thomas Stamford Raffles whose attention was drawn to one of the oddest flowers of all. This is the parasite that lives off the *tetrasigma* vine, an earth-trailing, ground-hogging liana-like growth found only in isolated pockets of the mountain forests of Sumatra and Borneo. Once every five years buds as big as cauliflowers bloom into enormous, leafless, science-fiction-style flowers consisting of five giant brown petals streaked with white, each flower measuring a metre in diameter and weighing up to nine kilos. Raffles' stopgap rule over what was then the Netherlands East Indies was an historical accident: Britain arbitrarily moved in, from 1811 to 1816, to pre-empt Napoleonic France's interest in the area. Such was the nineteenth-century reverence for colonial rulers, however ephemeral, that the flower was named 'Rafflesia'. Few people have ever seen this bizarre, carrion-scented flower, but Indonesia impinges on our daily lives far more than we realize: in furniture or panelling made of high-quality woods like camphor, ebony, and teak; in the spices we use such as pepper, cloves, nutmeg and chillies; in the tobacco, coffee, tea and cocoa we consume. And whereas other world producers of these commodities tend to concentrate their plantations into huge, integrated lots, the delight of Indonesia, and especially Java, is that it's all there in an abundant, checkerboard mix, banana trees adjacent to tea plantations, corncobs next to jackfruit.

Sheer diversity of this kind — tobacco bales next to baskets of tomatoes, spiced coconut delicacies cheek by jowl with baskets of tiny dried eels — is a characteristic feature of local shops. Few markets in Southeast Asia, not even the old, pre-war central markets of Saigon and Phnom Penh, can compare with the profusions on offer at the twice-weekly (Wednesdays and Saturdays) market in the hilltop town of Bukittinggi, Sumatra. Some of the exotic fruits are easily identifiable, such as the papaya, the spiky durian, the rose-red hairy rambutan. But several others are totally unfamiliar to Westerners, such as the *lengkeng*, the *salak*, the *blimbing*, the *nangka*, the *manggis*, the *jambu*, and the *bangkuang*. These are so completely unknown outside Indonesia, not because they 'fail to travel', like certain French wines from the southwest, but simply because they are essentially local produce, and not grown in sufficient quantities to merit the cost of airfreighting them abroad. Some, like the *salak*, with its snakeskin exterior, are natural works of art, even better to look at than eat. Others are indescribably delicious. Eaten raw and thinly sliced, the *bangkuang*, seems to the palate an unforgettable synthesis of melon and sweet potato. Even more exotic is the *timun suri,* with its flavors of cucumber and sweet melon, found mostly in Java.

And then, of course, there is rice. Like the Japanese, the Indonesians invest the cultivation of rice with a ritual, religious significance that goes far beyond its essential nutritive role. In parts of Bali, every small paddy-field has its own tiny shrine, the Rice God watching over her creation. Indonesian paddy-fields have a unique, ordered, vivid beauty, especially the 'wet' fields where each stalk is an essential component of a regimented, geometric whole — nature's inspiration to a Vasarély painting. In Java and Bali, Indonesia's main rice-growing areas, the soil is so rich and its farmers so skilled that, with the introduction of 'miracle' rice strains, three harvests a year have become possible. Even before, yields were the among the highest in the world. In the sixties, a time of wasted resources and unbelievable inflation, Indonesia was compelled to import 40% of its rice requirements. This is no longer necessary, despite its population of over 170 million, rising by 2.5 million a year. Because of the volcanic nature of the land, the rice fields of Java and Bali are never like the endlessly flat, green, billiard-

Manado, North Sulawesi: Still life with bamboo-handled *parang*, the Indonesian version of a machete, and a leather strap for keeping it sharp. **Mike Hosken, *New Zealand***

board expanses of China. They follow the contours of heady slopes. Some rice paddies are no more than a few feet wide, watery green strips hugging the hillside. It makes for back-breaking work: men and women tending the tiered rice paddies develop the leg muscles of cycling champions.

Implicit in the cultures of Indonesia's rice-growing areas is the complex communal water allocation system. Without the carefully timed damming of field after field in rigid sequence, rice cultivation on such a large scale would be impossible on a land where miniscule holdings predominate. The fair distribution of water often governs the complex web of social relations in a Javanese or Balinese village. Consensus is essential, hence the importance of farmers' irrigation societies, which work out water distribution plans, and their interlocking relations with village, family and neighborhood councils, and local administration. Even in areas where wet rice is not cultivated, there is a decidedly communal element to the way rural Indonesians organize themselves for the task of growing food, and for celebrating a successful harvest. This is why, whatever may be happening in the capital of Jakarta, grass-roots democracy is a given element of Indonesia's society. I asked one long-time foreign resident living in a remote village to give me her overriding impression of the community she had observed at close quarters for many years. The answer was unexpected: "It is," she said, "that I am among profoundly civilized people."

Yogyakarta, Central Java: Palace retainers of the *kraton* are the keepers of a rich court culture that has prevailed since the 18th century.
Gerald Gay, *Singapore*

Indonesia is so rich in natural resources that it's tempting to concentrate only on its preciously rare, unique phenomena: not just the 'Rafflesia' but also the giant lizards of Komodo, the dwarf buffaloes of Sulawesi, the Javanese rhinoceros and the now endangered gibbons and orangutangs. Indonesia's riches are not however, restricted to the esoteric. It is a major producer of tin, rubber, bauxite and timber, and a member of OPEC, of which the Sumatran, Kalimantan and Java oil-wells and offshore installations are a forceful reminder. The 'oil crisis' of 1973, which crippled so many countries, turned out to be a providential windfall for Indonesia. In comparison to many other developing countries, however, Indonesia has been more sophisticated: even in the middle of an economic boom, Indonesians remain conscious of their homeland's cultural values. Of course, their standard of living is important to them, as is the acquisition of the outward trappings of prosperity and modernity. What is unique is their ambivalence towards materialism. For most Indonesians, there are values so important that they are prepared to renounce, or delay, some degree of prosperity in order to safeguard them. Traditions, secular and religious, are not likely to go by the board, even if satellite dishes stud the remote countryside and the streets become clogged with new cars. This is perhaps the most surprising aspect of modern Indonesia. Here is a country that has moved from the status of colony to that of a modern, competitive industrial and agro-economic state without losing those characteristics which have been the first to be jettisoned in similar transformations elsewhere.

These riches are recognized only by specialists. For most Westerners, Indonesia's greatest resource is its coastline of endless beaches with every conceivable shade of sand, from white to orange to black, and a view from the shore of coconut trees on the atolls, and tiny specks of ocean-going 'prahus' whose shape has not changed substantially since the fifteenth century. Tourism is, of course, Indonesia's huge 'invisible' resource, but just how much of Indonesia does the tourist ever learn?

No rice paddy on Bali *(right)* is complete without a pair of water buffalo to plow the muddy plots – and a temple to ensure that the island's Hindu gods bless the fields with a bountiful harvest. A dugout canoe *(overleaf)* drifts down a tannic-colored tributary that winds through the marsh-lands of Irian Jaya's Casuarina Coast near Timika. This is a forbidding frontier, a hothouse of exotic creatures from glorious birds of paradise to longicorn beetles as big as birds.
G.A. Rossi, *Italy*
Bruno Barbey, *France*

ount
Bromo rises 2300
dramatic meters above
sea level then abruptly
plummets into a vast
smouldering crater of
smaller peaks and
gaping vents. On the
14th day of the last
month of their year,
the Tenggerese offer
gifts of vegetables and
chickens in the mid-
night chill, as they
have for centuries: it is
their dutiful gesture to
all the people of Java
who have traditionally
depended on them for
protection from the
terrible wrath of
Bromo.
Santoso Alimin,
Indonesia

Like the other islands of Nusa Tenggara, or Lesser Sundas, Sumbawa is drier and less fertile than islands to the west. The Lesser Sundas lie east of the Wallace Line, named for the 19th century naturalist and explorer. He plotted the line, an imaginary boundary between lush wet islands like Bali and Java and their distinctive plant and animal life, and the different flora and fauna of the other islands further east in the archipelago. Fish are something all have in common, however; Lake Mararan in eastern Sumbawa is a popular spot among anglers.

Ara Guler, *Turkey*

Clusters of tall bamboo dwarf a young man near Kambira in the Sangala area of South Sulawesi's Torajaland *(right)*. The Badui – who live a life apart deep in the mountains of West Java – prefer the old ways: they have straddled a river using hardy stalks of bamboo near the village of Gajebo *(top left)*. Meanwhile, in the interior of Seram in the Maluku, the isolated Maneo tribe cling to a primeval lifestyle – one of its archers uses a bamboo arrow to hunt game for a meal *(bottom left)*.

Dominic Sansoni,
Sri Lanka
Desi Harahap,
Indonesia
Rio Helmi, *Indonesia*

Incessant tropical rains water the lush forests that blanket the mountain realm of West Java's Badui people, effectively insulating their ancient culture from the 20th century. The Badui shun electric appliances, engines and other modern conveniences; in the village of Gajeboh, big banana leafs and a wide-brimmed palm-weave hat serve as umbrellas.

Desi Harahap, *Indonesia*

A

creeper vine snakes
into the tree tops on
Handeleum Island
one of two
waystations for
expeditions to the
immense Ujung Kulon
National Park on the
southwestern tip of
Java, the last refuge of
the island's elusive
white rhinoceros.
Lombok, east of Bali,
has some of the most
spectacular geology
on the planet. One of
Lombok's attractions is
the Sindeniggile
waterfall which gushes
from a volcanic cliff
wall.
Leo Meier, *Australia*
Mike Yamashita, *USA*

irds and butterflies thrive in the islands, adding innumerable splashes of color to the perpetual shadows of the rain forests. In the Ujung Kulon National Park in West Java, a large hornbill that the Indonesians call *engrang* finds a comfortable perch *(left)*. Meanwhile, far to the east in the village of Uldam in Irian Jaya's Baliem Valley a *kupukupu*, Indonesian for butterfly, finds an even more comfortable spot – the forehead of Andarias Pridoman *(right)*.
Leo Meier, *Australia*
Robin Moyer, *USA*

Board a dugout canoe *(extreme lower left)* and navigate past river mangroves *(extreme lower right)* up the myriad rivers and tributaries of Central Kalimantan; or pull on your boots and trek into the tropical rain forests of the immense Ujung Kulon National Park. But step carefully: underfoot are all manner of deadly snakes, lazy lizards, curious toads, giant spiders and beetles, and tiny monkeys; and new species are constantly being discovered.

Martin Kers, *Netherlands* (2)

Leo Meier, *Australia* (7)

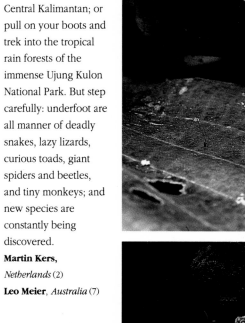

G ibbons, or *lutung (left and right);* just one of 500 varieties of mammals among the archipelago's fauna. Far removed from the rest of the world, in rugged seas between Sumbawa and Flores, evolution on Komodo Island *(overleaf)* seems to have taken its own course. The Komodo dragon is an aggressive creature that can measure more than three meters and weigh 100 kilograms.
Leo Meier, *Australia*
Mahendra Sinh, *India*
Peter Hufgard, *New Zealand*

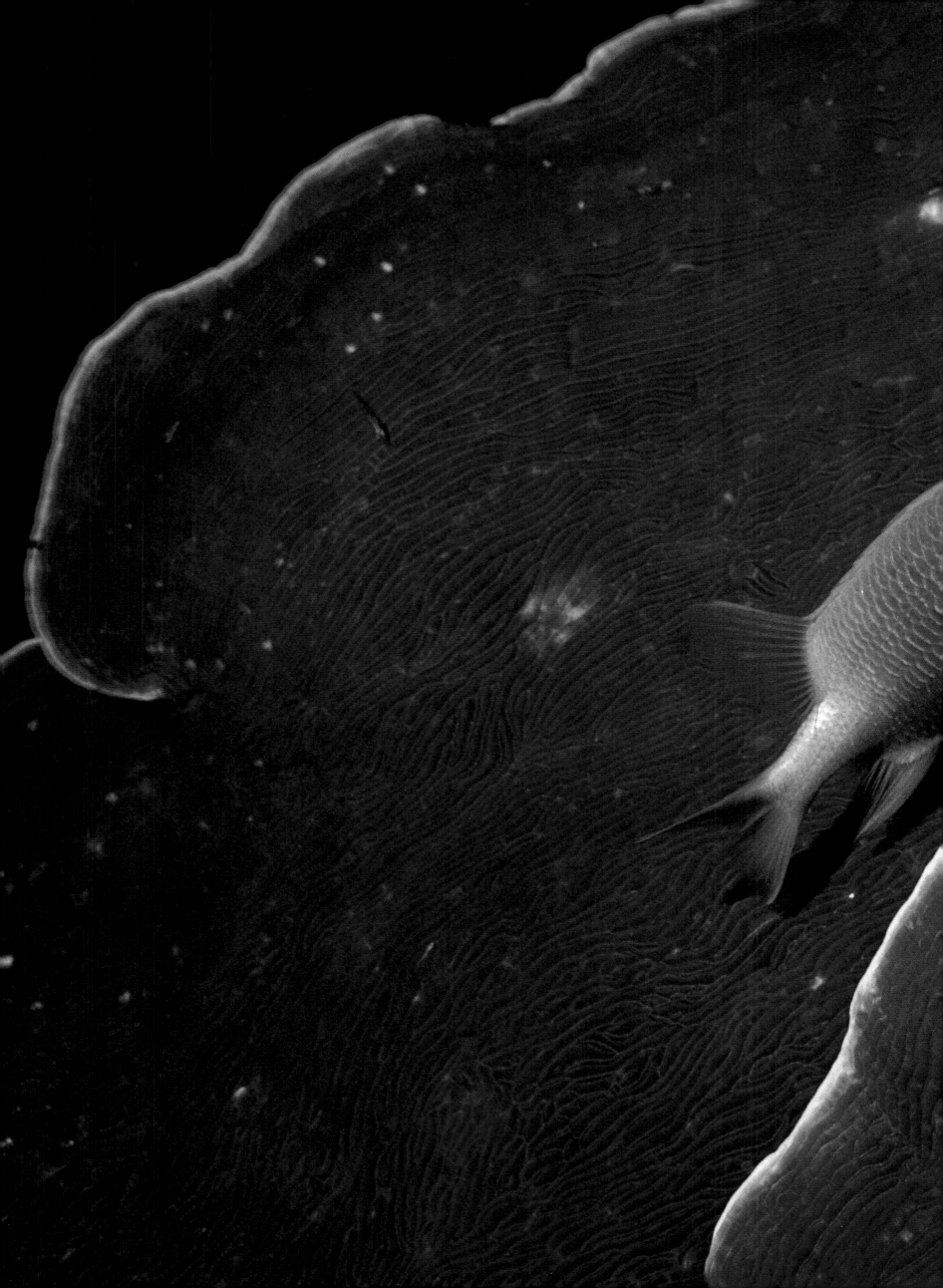

On any given day, any given dive into the transparent waters of the archipelago may produce a face-to-face encounter with a representative of Indonesia's exotic marine life. Fantastic coral and nearly three hundred feet of visibility make the diving in Cendrawasih Bay off of Irian Jaya among the very best in the world *(this page and overleaf)*. The tepid, placid waters off Santana Beach near Dili, *(further overleaf)* are a good place to go in search of a fresh catch to sell at the morning market. Against the East Timor hills and the silhouette of handsome coastal vessels, a lone fisherman wearing a palm weave basket on his back in expectation of a big haul expertly casts his net.

Andre Pribadi, *Indonesia* (10)

Tara Sosrowardojo, *Indonesia*

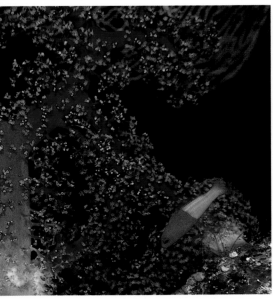
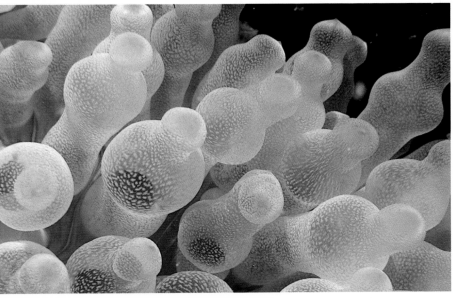
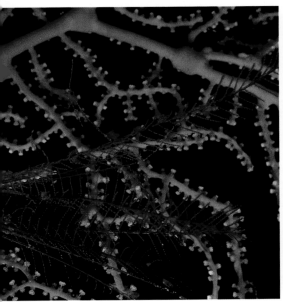

Art, music, color and Bali are four magic words that are practically synonomous: Even fisherman off Bali transform their fleet into an explosive symphony of visual excitement, one that any self-respecting fish would be proud to be caught by.

G. A. Rossi, *Italy*

Indonesia's 13,000 islands offer miles of coastline, palm-fringed, or mangrove-edged or rocky and dramatic like this nearly-deserted beach in Lombok *(right)*. Indonesia's beaches are a Westerner's romantic dream, and across the archipelago new developments are catering to the tourist hunger for sun and sea. A Balinese fishing outrigger has been fitted with an outboard *(left)* and turned into a day-tripping dive boat.
Mike Yamashita, *USA*
G. A. Rossi, *Italy*

I t's not the only way to travel in South Kalimantan – but a boat or canoe is often the only way to get where you're going. Two young women on Lake Tahai *(right)* resort to paddlepower. There are treasures deep in the tropical forest, and these miners in South Kalimantan are willing to put up with a lot of mud in their search for diamonds. The name Kalimantan may derive from the words "river of diamonds".

Martin Kers, *Netherlands*

An oil exploration rig called Ternate belonging to Total, a French company involved in a local joint venture, does some test drilling in East Kalimantan's Mahakam River delta *(left).* A helicopter pad and docking facilities are standard equipment for rigs working onshore or offshore. Indonesia's rich deposits of oil and natural gas provide petrodollars to fuel the country's development. Now there is a growing emphasis on diversifying Indonesia's industrial base.

Georg Gerster,
Switzerland

G. A. Rossi, *Italy*

Logjams occur frequently on East Kalimantan's Mahakam River, especially near Tenggarong *(right),* where logs cut from giant hardwoods in timber concessions upriver are guided downstream by make-shift houseboats. Downriver the logs will be loaded onto freighters, like this one *(bottom left)* from Jakarta. The river is East Kalimantan's main thoroughfare: ships of all shapes and sizes crowd its mouth at Samarinda, including the small riverboats *(top left)* that ferry people and goods into the interior.

Georg Gerster, *Switzerland*
Kal Muller, *USA*

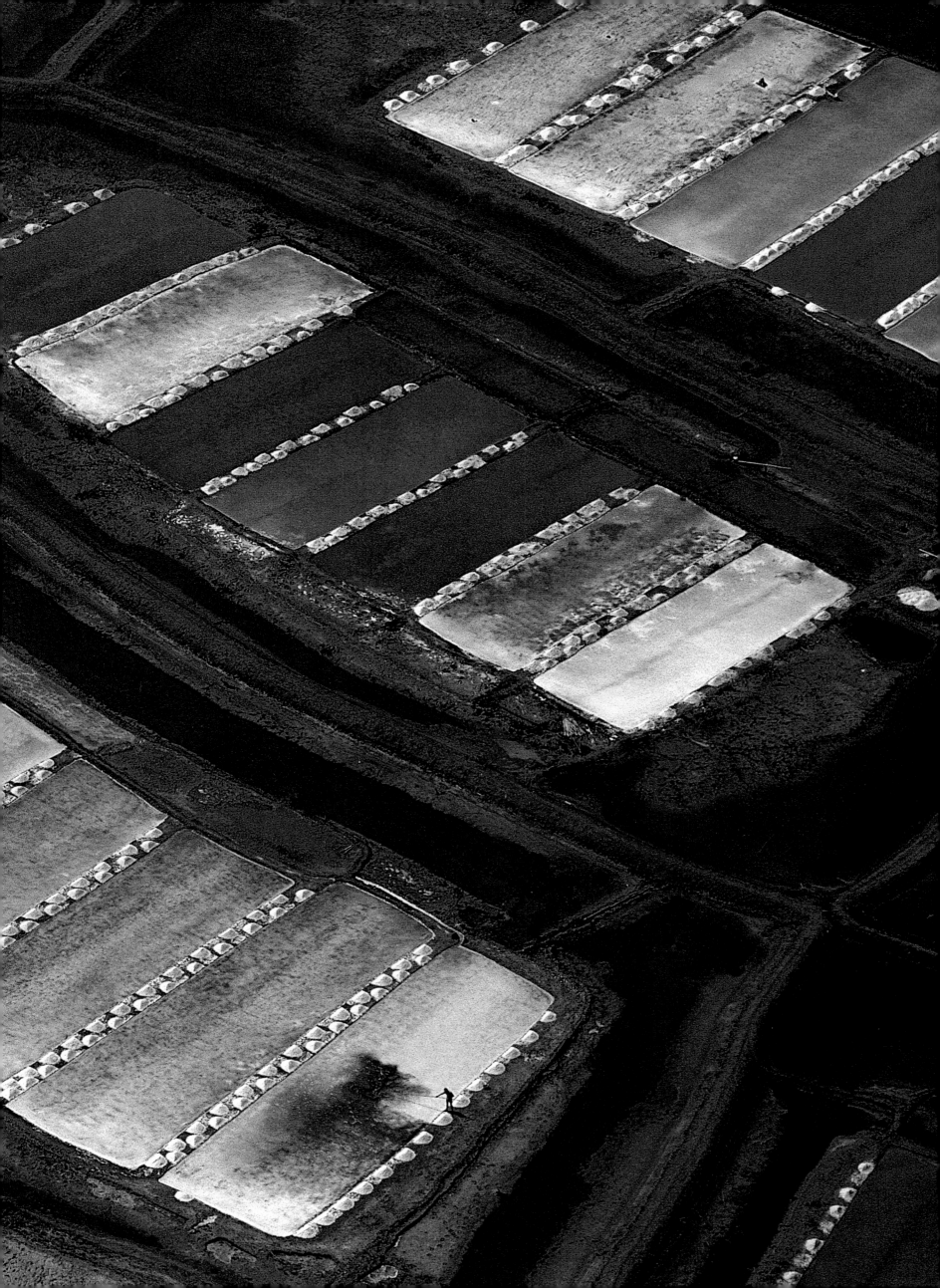

Work in the fields is often best done communally. These villagers are preparing a field for planting near the village of Bima on Sumbawa island. In contrast to the lush beauty of terraced fields when seen from the air, saltworks cut stark abstracts into the island of Madura *(overleaf)*, just across a narrow strait from Surabaya, East Java. The condiment is "harvested" from the coastal marshes, dried in the sun on immense pans, then scraped into small piles for packing; the industry has been crucial to the island for at least three centuries.
Ara Guler, *Turkey*
Georg Gerster,
Switzerland

With the right amount of hard work, Indonesian earth can be made to nourish crops like these: tea *(top left)* in West Java, rice in Sumatra *(bottom left),* and fruits like the *nangka* or jackfruit in Bali *(right).* Even foreboding fields high in Bali's volcanos are fertile enough for cultivation *(preceding).* This woman passes a freshly-watered field after an exhilirating shampoo in the waters of Lake Batur, Bali's largest lake.

Peter van der Velde, *Netherlands*
Ian Berry, *UK*
Mike Yamashita, *USA*
Raghu Rai, *India*

Some Sasaks, the Muslim majority of the island of Lombok, inhabit highland villages like this one near Cakranegara. Their traditional dwellings – made from timber, woven bamboo and palm-leaf thatch – display a towering roofline common to the diverse peoples of the many islands of eastern Indonesia.

Mike Yamashita, *USA*

When the tide is high, stilts keep the homes of Bajao fisherman dry although the chickens in the front yard may have to do a duck walk to avoid getting their feathers' wet. Life in small villages like this one north of Maumere on Flores is governed by the ebb and flow of the tides, the phases of the moon and the rising and setting sun. Off Batam island a molten equatorial sunset *(overleaf)* burnishes the balmy waters within rowing distance of Singapore, fishermen head out in search of their evening catch against the silhouette of a *kelong,* a structure used to snare fish and shellfish in long tunnel-nets.
Michael Freeman, *UK*
Koes, *Indonesia*

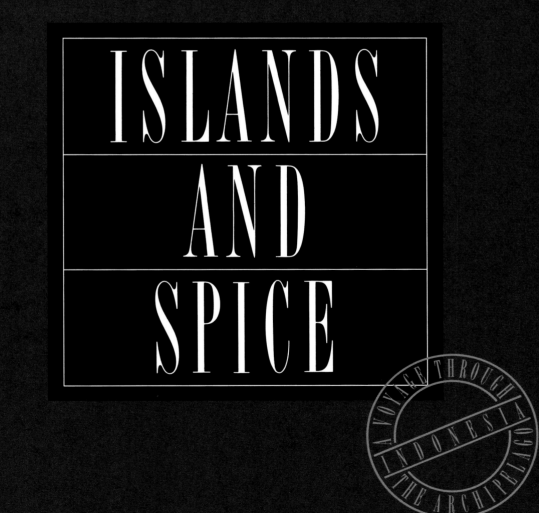

The mist-shrouded Dieng Plateau in central Java is a magical spot. Tiered rice paddies give way to steep-banked potato fields rising layer by layer to 1200 meters in one of the most mysterious, volcanic landscapes on earth. Temperatures are cool but the traditionally clad peasants go barefoot. There are few tourists, no telephones, no souvenir stands. Access is limited to one narrow, winding mountain road. Billowing steam marks the presence of several boiling craters, the black churning wells of scalding water that are a constant reminder of the threat of volcanic eruption over Java.

In the plain below are four lovingly preserved Hindu temple ruins. On the altarbase inside (all that remains is the *yoni*; the *lingam* has long since disappeared) are scattered flower petals, signs that Hindu worshippers still come here. Yet, at sunrise and sunset, the plateau reverberates with the electronically amplified 'muezzin', the hypnotic Islamic call to prayer. Three hours drive away is Borobudur, site of possibly the most imposing monument to Mahayana Buddhism. At nightfall, this dark, sleepy town also echoes to the muezzin. There is no street lighting but the glow of TV sets from every roadside living room.

The sound is as incongruous as it would be in the vicinity of the Vatican or Saint Paul's cathedral, and it could not happen anywhere else but in Indonesia where animism, Buddhism, Hinduism, Islam and Christianity not only coexist, but seem to have drawn inspiration from each other. Before this could occur, however, there would be centuries of intermittent warfare between rival Hindu, Buddhist and later Islamic rulers across the archipelago. The conflicts, however violent, never took the form of religious wars, or *jihads*. Rather, the various religious factions were motivated by inevitable earthly ambitions: here were some of the richest spice-producing islands in the world, up for grabs at a time when spices were almost worth their weight in gold. No wonder Hindus, Buddhists and Islams took their turn in dominating parts of Indonesia. More surprisingly, freedom of worship was never in question, at least not until the arrival of the missionary, who came in the wake of the entrepreneurial Portuguese and the Dutch. Religious intolerance, and the arrogant white certitude that everything European was best, were later features of colonial rule, especially in the Moluccas.

The proliferation of Hindu and Buddhist temples in Java, and fine examples of Hindu art at first led historians to believe that a fully-fledged Indian invasion must have occurred there in the first few centuries AD. This theory has been thoroughly discredited, now that detailed studies have revealed traces of pre-Hindu techniques, styles and craftsmanship unknown in India. The current conventional wisdom is that India colonized Java culturally and artistically, but peaceably, through trade and civilized intercourse. Local Javanese aristocrats, it is thought, were so impressed by Indian affluence, lifestyle and the intrinsic lure of Hinduism and Buddhism, that they quite deliberately began adapting India's customs to their own. Hindu-Buddhist religion, culture and art were not imposed but assimilated.

The islands' heritage rests in the hands of an older generation, like this woman weaver from the island of Flores. Years of indigo-dying have stained her skin, in contrast to the creamy sheen of her ivory bangles, heirlooms made from elephant tusks traded many years ago from islands to the west.
Michael Freeman, *UK*

According to archaeological evidence, Buddhism was already a force in Java in these early days. In the seventh century the Buddhist Srivijaya dynasty, based in Palembang, southern Sumatra, dominated the incense trade with China and continued to rule for the next six hundred years. Theirs was a curious empire, a loosely linked network of trading centres and allied cities that stretched at times to Thailand and Indochina. Doubtless one of the world's great cities around 1100 AD, Srivijaya attracted Buddhist pilgrims from China and Vietnam, India and Japan, and from even further afield. While the Srivijayan empire disintegrated slowly over the next four hundred years, it left behind a tradition of domination of the archipelago that was to inspire its heirs, including the famous sea gypsies, formidable floating populations that considered piracy a highly respectable way of life.

The Srivijayans, despite their wealth and the reach of their seaborne power, were seemingly never able to dominate — at least not for any length of time — the richest of the islands, and the one closest to Sumatra: Java. Java was itself the bone of contention of another set of Buddhist kings, the Sailendras, in the eighth and ninth centuries. During this time the Buddhist temple, Borobudur, one of the wonders of the world, was built by an army of craftsmen over a period of seventy-five years or more. It was not so much a temple as a place of pilgrimage and meditation, and a Mahayana Buddhist university where would-be monks studied for enlightenment. Other temples, equally impressive as Borobudur, were built in the fertile central Javanese plain by the Sanjayas, a Hindu succession of rulers. A century later, this incredibly creative outburst ceased. The recent discovery of the Sambisari temple near Yogyakarta has suggested that a massive volcanic eruption caused a shift in population, to East Java.

The centuries that followed were marked by ding-dong battles in Java between the Buddhist and Hindu descendants of the old Sanjaya dynasty. Kublai Khan sent a Chinese ambassador to Java in 1289, who came demanding tribute and instead received

Suaya-Sanggala, Torajaland, South Sulawesi: Here one is never far from the regard of the ancestors: carvings called *tau-tau* stare out from burial caves.
Dominic Sansoni,
Sri Lanka

horrible disfigurement for his arrogance. As a result the Mongol Emperor sent an expeditionary force to Java in 1293. A pro-Chinese coalition of Buddhist and local rulers helped it initially to victory, but the Chinese later fled in disarray when their erstwhile allies, led by the shrewd Prince Vijaya, turned against them.

The end of the thirteenth and beginning of the fourteenth centuries witnessed the emergence of the Majapahit kingdom. Now, for the first time, a Javanese power set about dominating what is now known as Indonesia. They established trading centres in the easternmost islands, swept away the vestiges of Srivijayan power in Sumatra, and clashed with an aggressive Siam up and down the Malay peninsula.

However, the Majapahit kingdom declined in a welter of family quarrels, and meanwhile Islam was proving itself to be a new dynamic force in the area. Around the turn of the fifteenth century, principalities on the north coast of central Java such as Cirebon, Demak and Jepara, were under Islamic rulers. Both Hindu and Buddhist rajas and kings, united in defeat, fled eastward to Bali with their priests, dancing girls, cooks and retainers. The masses left behind became Muslims, while in Bali Hinduism prevailed, though in a more exuberant, tolerant and polymorphous form, incorporating the pre-Hindu animism that still predominates in parts of Bali today.

Rantepao, Torajaland, South Sulawesi: Exotic to the foreign eye, for this Toraja man, the colors and ornament of his festive outfit are everyday life.
Dominic Sansoni, *Sri Lanka*

Islamic domination of the Indonesian archipelago reached its peak in the fifteenth and sixteenth centuries, but no single, unifying kingdom emerged. Most of Java came under Islamic rule but the rulers remained divided, while in northern Sumatra, the Achenese had become doggedly, fanatically Muslim and separatist. As Indonesia was flourishing through profitable trading in spices with India, China, and the Middle East, it was inevitable that other, more remote seafaring nations should seek a piece of the action. By the sixteenth century a new and far more lethal set of invaders now appeared on Indonesian shores: the Portuguese, then the Dutch, who, at first with the Dutch East India Company, then with a fully fledged colonial government, started turning as much of Indonesia as they could control into a profitable, monopolistic spice preserve, based on forcible expropriation and slave labor. Cloves, hugely in demand all over the world, became at first a Portuguese and then a Dutch monopoly, enforced at terrible human cost, and with restricted production to keep prices fraudulently high.

The conquest was hugely lucrative but costly: time and again Javanese sultans and Sulawesi kings faced colonial troops with suicidal fury. A war with the tough Achenese dragged on from the 1870s for nearly thirty years, the Dutch enlisting mercenaries in a foreign-legion-type army to do their dirty work. By the late nineteenth century they had triumphed: Batavia, later Jakarta, was to all intents a Dutch town, with canals and narrow, wooden houses reminiscent of Amsterdam; an all-powerful Governor-General ruled in Sumatra, Kalimantan and Sulawesi, and Dutch colonial officers elsewhere acted as 'advisers' to local rulers, in effect exercizing authority in their name.

Ex-colonial empires have a tendency towards mutual admiration and idealization. Victor Purcell, the late Cambridge historian, regarded the urban administration of the early twentieth-century Netherlands East Indies as 'a model of efficiency', disapproving only its 'excessive paternalism'. An American writer Eliza Ruhama, an indomitable traveller, is more scathing: in 1899 she wrote of the "abject crouching (Javanese) humility before their Dutch employers" and noted that "the brutality of the latter to them is a theme for sadder thinking, and calculated to make the blood boil". What shocked her most was the contrast between the puritanical, thrifty, prudish Dutch in their native Holland and their "blooming out in the forcing house of the tropics into strange laxity", and the sight of "(native) women lolling barefooted and in startling dishabille in splendid equipages...there in the hotel was an undress parade that beggars description...bare-ankled women, clad only in a sarong and white dressing jacket, go unconcernedly about their affairs in streets and public places. It is a dishabille beyond all burlesque pantomime." She was most shocked by the prevalence of 'mixed couples'. Unlike British India, where strict segregation was the rule, extra-marital and interracial liaisons were common, at least until 1900. The Dutch could not resist the attractions of the dainty, lissome Javanese women. Here too colonialism had its ugly side, for once they became *nyai*, or concubines, they had no rights whatever. Their children were taken from them and they could be abandoned with no compensation whenever their masters tired of them.

The Indonesian archipelago was so vast, its people so different, that no colonial system could hope to impose a single regime throughout the islands, and indeed for some of them its impact was slight. Access was simply too difficult, the diversity of its indigenous inhabitants unmanageable. The oldest islanders — negritos, Australoids, and proto-Malays — were once thought to have colonized the area in successive waves. Ethnologists no longer believe this, and the likeliest theory is that trade, travel and inter-marriage across the islands account for Indonesia's racial and cultural mix. Some basic questions remain: how do the people of the Nias, an island off the northwest coast of Sumatra, belong to the same language group as the Samoans in the distant Pacific? Why did the once animist Bataks of Sumatra (whom the Dutch mistakenly regarded as savages) become such devout Christians, while still treasuring their distinctly non-Christian animist beliefs and traditions? What compelled the Minangkabau, the inhabitants of West Sumatra, to become one of the few matrilinear societies in the world,

Makale, Torajaland, South Sulawesi: Women mourners at funerals here swathe themselves in black from head to toe.
Dominic Sansoni, *Sri Lanka*

to the extent that land is owned by women, and husbands call on their wives at the latters' behest? Odder still, why did the Minangkabau, with their complicated clan rules, become Muslims, albeit of a maverick kind, and how did they reconcile Islamic laws with those of their own, distinctly non-Islamic society?

The questions become even more unanswerable as one moves eastward. Yogyakarta is in many respects a bustling twentieth-century town, Indonesia's batik center, a thriving commercially-inclined metropolis where 'Dallas' and 'Dynasty' (dubbed in Bahasa Indonesia) are ever-popular television programs — not on the face of it the most promising place for the study of traditional Hindu and Buddhist historical and religious legends. Yet, for all its modern veneer, Yogyakarta's FM radio stations transmit the interminable shadow puppet theatre plays, the *wayang kulit*, throughout the night. These are followed religiously by hundreds of thousands of Javanese who delight in the endless retelling of the 'Mahabharata' myths which they already know by heart.

Bawomataluwo, Nias: The people of Nias – and many other Indonesians – face a great challenge in adapting to new ways of life, as economic growth and development challenge the roots of their traditional cultures. **Darwis Triadi,** *Indonesia*

In Bali, art and religion are not solely the domain of the experts, but are everyone's business. Even in bustling villages transformed by tourism, funeral rites and temple ceremonies can bring all commercial activity to a halt for days at a time, and in each village the gamelan ensemble and dance troupe perform whether or not there are tourists there to watch. The village feast, which wards off evil spirits, is as routine as a rotarian lunch, and small children become apprentice musicians or dancers by the time they are five years old. Ironically, Bali, the island now synonymous with Indonesian tourism, was once completely isolated. The Balinese found solace in their rich earth but feared the ocean surrounding them. Until the mid 1920s, foreigners were distrusted and not particularly welcome. It is a miracle that, for all the ravages of modern tourism, the Balinese have not lost their soul: social bonds remain strong, and off the beaten tourist track, life still revolves around the three obligatory temples maintained by each village, around their communal meeting places, kitchens and percussion orchestras, above all around the rituals of dance.

Bali has an artificial, luxurious playground in its southernmost tip: Nusa Dua is for those who want to enjoy all its amenities without ever coming face to face with its people other than as servants, dancers or gamelan orchestra members performing in hotel lobbies. But any Balinese dirt-track leads eventually to a village with walled temples and elaborate carvings, and every neighborhood has its own musical and dance repertoire, its set of household gods and patrons, and is surprisingly self-sufficient. Visitors are welcome because hospitality is a virtue, but the Balinese do not rely on tourist revenue to finance expensive dance costumes, ritual banquets and time-consuming religious rites. Everyone contributes. Foreigners cannot hope to understand the intricacies of religious festivals without years of study, but the pulsating sound of the gamelan percussion orchestra, with its unwritten, ever-evolving rhythms, is accessible to us all. It reminds one that within every Balinese household there is an artistic tradition, and that while the lives of many straddle both the Western and Balinese worlds, it is their own, hermetic culture which remains essential to them.

As in so much of Indonesia, one can only wonder at the strength of local traditions, which have survived wars, natural calamities, colonial oppression, a state of near civil war and — perhaps the most insidious onslaught of all — the temptation to turn these artistic gifts into marketable assets in a world where profit has become the latest household god.

A bright smile – well-protected from an even brighter sun, lights up this young Jakarta boy's face. **Paul Chesley,** *USA*

A
Javanese man raises his eyes to the heavens *(preceding)* and revels in his religion: faith is a transcendent experience for Indonesians. The vast majority answer to the call of Islam. Pancasila, the nation's political creed, also recognises the Christian, Hindu and Buddhist faiths, and Indonesians have evolved a unique kind of religious toleration over the years. One of the first areas in Java to undergo the transition to Islam was the cosmopolitan northern coast. In this mosque in the north central town of Demak, the latest gossip elicits hardy laughter. Between prayers, mosques become a focal point for communal activities as well as religious functions. Some mosques in Demak are among Java's oldest.
G Pinkhassov, *USSR*
Steve Vidler, *UK*

Muslim women wear special white robes when at prayer *(left)*. Indonesia encompasses a vast variety of doctrines and degrees of the Islamic faith; after all it has the world's largest population of Muslims. Within Indonesia, the people of Aceh *(right)* are known for their faith and adherence to Islamic law. Aceh was once a major staging point for Muslims on their way to Mecca from all over maritime Asia.

G Pinkhassov, *USSR*

Ian Berry, *UK*

Young Muslim women wear their religion proudly as they pray at Sultan Fateh mosque in Demak, the center of a 16th century Muslim kingdom in Central Java. This solemn group, covered from head-to-toe in the traditional white *telekong*, finger prayer beads while saying the Zikir, a practice of the Qadyirah branch of Sufi Muslims in which worshipers chant holy phrases 1000 times.
Abbas, *France*

A Javanese woman reads from the Koran *(right)* at the tomb of Sunan Kudus, in the central Java city of Kudus. In the 15th century, the Sunan Kudus built this mosque on the site of a Hindu temple, and it has been revered as a place of pilgrimage ever since. It takes intense concentration to memorise the Koran in Arabic, especially when your mother tongue is Bahasa Indonesia. But for these three boys in the East Java village of Gramatayu *(left)* it is a sacred duty and an integral part of their upbringing.
Abbas, *France*

In Java, Islam coexists with a whole complex of beliefs and practices called *kejawen,* literally Javanism *(left).* In Imogiri, Central Java, pilgrims don traditional Javanese garb and pray at royal tombs of the Yogya and Solo lines *(right).* From above, the massive majesty of Central Java's Borobudur *(overleaf)* is awesome: more so in light of the fact that the architects who built it a thousand years ago never had the means to view their masterpiece from this perspective.

Bruno Barbey, *France*
Georg Gerster, *Switzerland*

Pancasila, Indonesia's state philosophy, professes a belief in one God but underscores the freedom of worship. A stone carver's showroom in Central Java provides a vivid example of how various faiths can exist peacefully, side by side *(top)*. The province of East Timor, long a Portuguese colony, remains a stronghold of Catholicism *(bottom);* note the finely-carved statue of the Virgin Mary held by this woman in the village of Vemasse. The same spirit of sanctity is seen in this nun at one of East Timor's many churches.

Abbas, *France*

Tara Sosrowardojo (2), *Indonesia*

Balinese women in festive dress propitiate the gods and make their colorful Galungan offerings at a temple in the Badung area. Rice cakes, fruits and other delights are stacked in front of altars that have been decorated with intricate palm-leaf cut-outs called *lamak.* Galungan, one of an almost endless succession of festivals in Bali, marks the beginning of a 42-day holy period which includes another major holiday called Kuningan. Tanah Lot temple *(preceding)* is one of Bali's most dramatic: at low tide worshippers walk through the shallows to the temple despite the reputation of the black seasnakes which live in the surrounding rocks and caves.
Raghu Rai, *India*

Like its counterpart in India, Balinese Hinduism is a rich heady mix of beliefs, doctrine, festivals and local tradition. Offerings to the spirits of the unseen world are an important part of both daily life and special occasions, like this wedding in the princely house of Karangasem *(top left)* or a special purification ceremony *(right)*. Priests *(below left)* of different caste serve on family occasions or for temple ceremonies which occur in a 210-day cycle.

David Bowie, *UK*

Raghu Rai, *India*

hinese
religion is a complex
mix of Buddhism and
Chinese beliefs and
philosophies: The
religion of Indonesia's
Chinese preserves
some of the practices
and cults now lost to
China's mainland. The
religion is ruled by the
lunar calendar, and the
basic act of propi-
tiation involves
burning incense and
bowing to a Boddhi-
sattva or saint, asking
them for a special
blessing.
Leong Ka Tai,
Hong Kong

Indonesia's Chinese minority is small but plays a big role in the economy. Chinese communities in towns large and small are assimilating into the Indonesian mainstream, but still maintain links with their cultural traditions. The old center of the community is the temple, like the Vihara Bumi Raya in Pemangkat. Modern and traditional mix in a home in the Chinatown quarter of Padang in West Sumatra – the family altar right above the family television set. On a grander scale, but equally eclectic, is the Maimoon Palace in Medan, North Sumatra *(overleaf)*. It was designed by an Italian architect in 1888.
Leong Ka Tai, *Hong Kong,*
Basil Pao, *Hong Kong*
Eddy Posthuma deBoers, *Netherlands*

The latest in the royal line of Yogyakarta sultans is Hamengkubuwono X. The sultanate dates back to the 18th century – when the once mighty Mataram empire had been divided between the noble houses of Yogya and Solo. Here, the Sultan and his wife strike a regal pose in the *kraton* or palace. The *kraton* today *(right)* are opened to tourists like the stately homes of Europe. Unlike their European counterparts however, Java's *kraton* are still considered very important by many as sites for rituals and religious observances.

Luca I. Tettoni, *Italy*

The curves of the *keris* are a triumph of the blacksmith's art. Made from iron and meteoric nickel, the most famous *keris* are believed to have magical powers and personalities. An essential part of the formal dress of a Javanese man, some fine *keris* are also royal regalia, with important ceremonial roles. Here in the Mangkunegaran *kraton* in Solo courtiers make offerings to the *keris* and clean it with lime juice, oil, and in a new innovation, a little Brasso. Aside from doing honor to the *keris,* this cleaning brings out the patterns of the incredibly fine damascene of the blade.

Luca I. Tettoni, *Italy*

It is weddings that bring out the best in Indonesia's cultures: elegant costumes, genteel ceremony – and delicious cuisine. No guest could go home hungry: a Minangkabau family lays on a typical spread at their home near West Sumatra's Lake Singkarak *(right)*. The bridal "shower" takes on a quite literal meaning in the prelude to a Javanese wedding. Isna, the daughter of Soedjatmoko, Indonesia's ex-ambassador to the US, takes a deep breath as a relative douses her with water during a cleansing and purification ritual that took place in the bride's home in Jakarta's stately Menteng suburb.
Basil Pao, *Hong Kong*
Star Black, *USA*

A dancer of Yogyakarta's *kraton*: *(right)* the embellished curves of her headress blend flawlessly with the contours of her exquisite features. The same spirit moves the puppets of the *wayang golek* – their wooden expressions *(left)* give way to lifelike gestures when animated by their *dalang* or puppet-master. In *wayang golek* plays, epic sagas provide a vast cast *(overleaf)* of kings, queens, jokers, warriors, spirits and monsters.

Fendi Siregar, *Indonesia*
Luca I. Tettoni, *Italy*
Bruno Barbey, *France*

Java's shadow puppet plays, the *wayang kulit,* remain popular as entertainment today. Equally entertaining is this encounter between tourists and Indonesians: producing good vibrations at Pak Ujo's *angklung* school in Bandung *(left).* Visitors are handed one of the bamboo instruments, get the signal when to shake it and, voila! instantly become a key component in an *angklung* orchestra right alongside Sundanese youngsters. **Fendi Siregar** (2), *Indonesia* **Luca I. Tettoni,** *Italy*

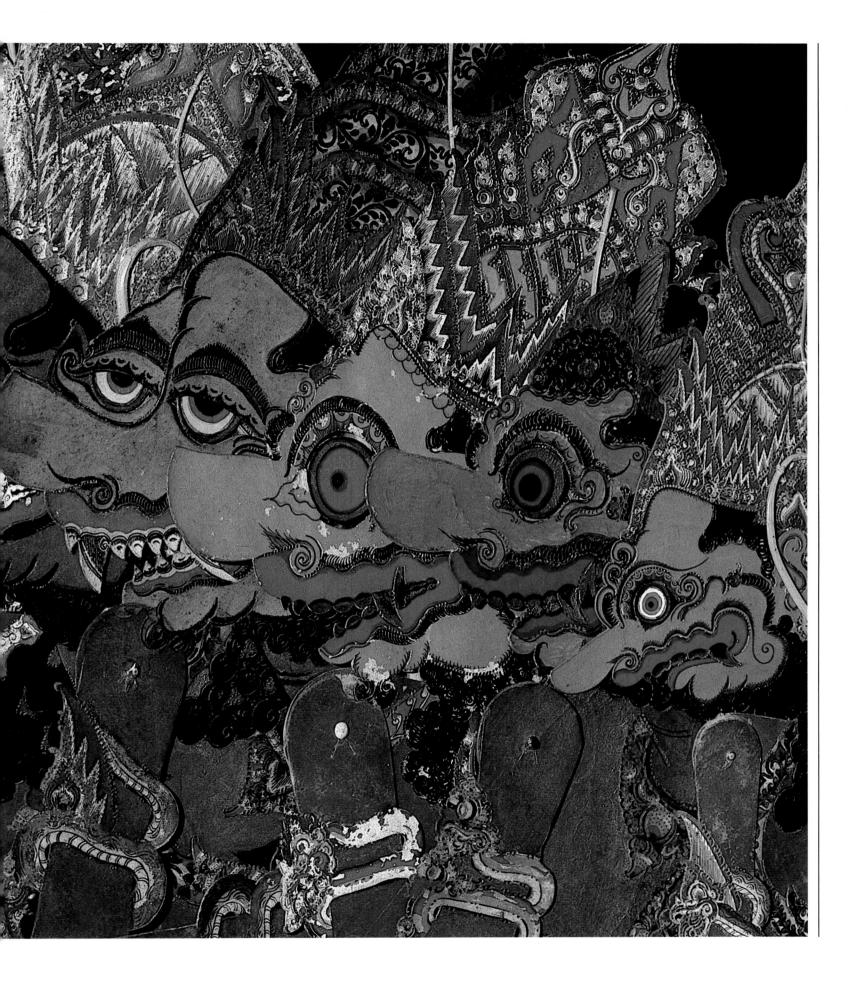

In Bali, everyone is a performer. The arts are serious business for people from all walks of life. The education of a Balinese dancer begins at an early age; so too learning the rudiments of the fine art of primping for the night's big rehearsal. Getting the hair styled just right is crucial – and an extra large comb certainly helps. While less integrated into everyday life than Balinese dance and drama, popular street opera and theater – the *stamboul* – is very much alive in towns and villages throughout the rest of Indonesia. Elaborate costumes, dancing and acrobatics, all to the tune of a gamelan or *gong* ensemble, turn performances like these in Central Java and Lombok into grand spectacle *(preceding and overleaf)*.
Paul Chesley, *USA*
G Pinkhassov, *USSR*
Mike Yamashita, *USA*

W here there are Indonesians, there's almost always art, often – though not always – masterful. In Kasongan *(top right)*, outside of Yogyakarta, the local artists work with the most fundamental element, earth. Another Yogya area craftsman *(bottom right)* carves *wayang golek* puppets, and his spectacles – one can only suppose – give him a keener eye for their character. An art form too are kites, and flying them is a popular sport. This Sasak villager *(left)* on the island of Lombok is creating a large kite from natural materials.
G. Pinkhassov (2), *USSR*
Mike Yamashita, *USA*

Island scenes: The influence of Balinese culture on neighboring Lombok is apparent in the *wayang* war being waged above the head of this youngster at Sweta market *(top right)*. She's got the look; he's got the time *(bottom right)*. After a protracted struggle against separatists, East Timor is returning to normal; This doorstep fronts a painted wall in Dili, the capital. A young woman of Flores *(left)* wraps herself in a sarong woven in the ikat technique typical of Nusa Tenggara.
Mike Yamashita, *USA*
Tara Sosrowardjojo, *Indonesia*
Michael Freeman, *UK*

The Indonesian version of a bullfight: this animal has exerted a special fascination over the centuries in places as far afield as Southeast Asia, India, China, and Southern Europe. The Madurese, separated from East Java by a narrow strait, are fond of bull races. These are grand occasions, and the bulls are specially bred for speed and trained for their vocation. The races offer plenty of thrills and spills, for the bull drivers ride precarious light wooden sledges that seem to fly behind the speedy bull-team. **Richard Kalvar,** *USA*

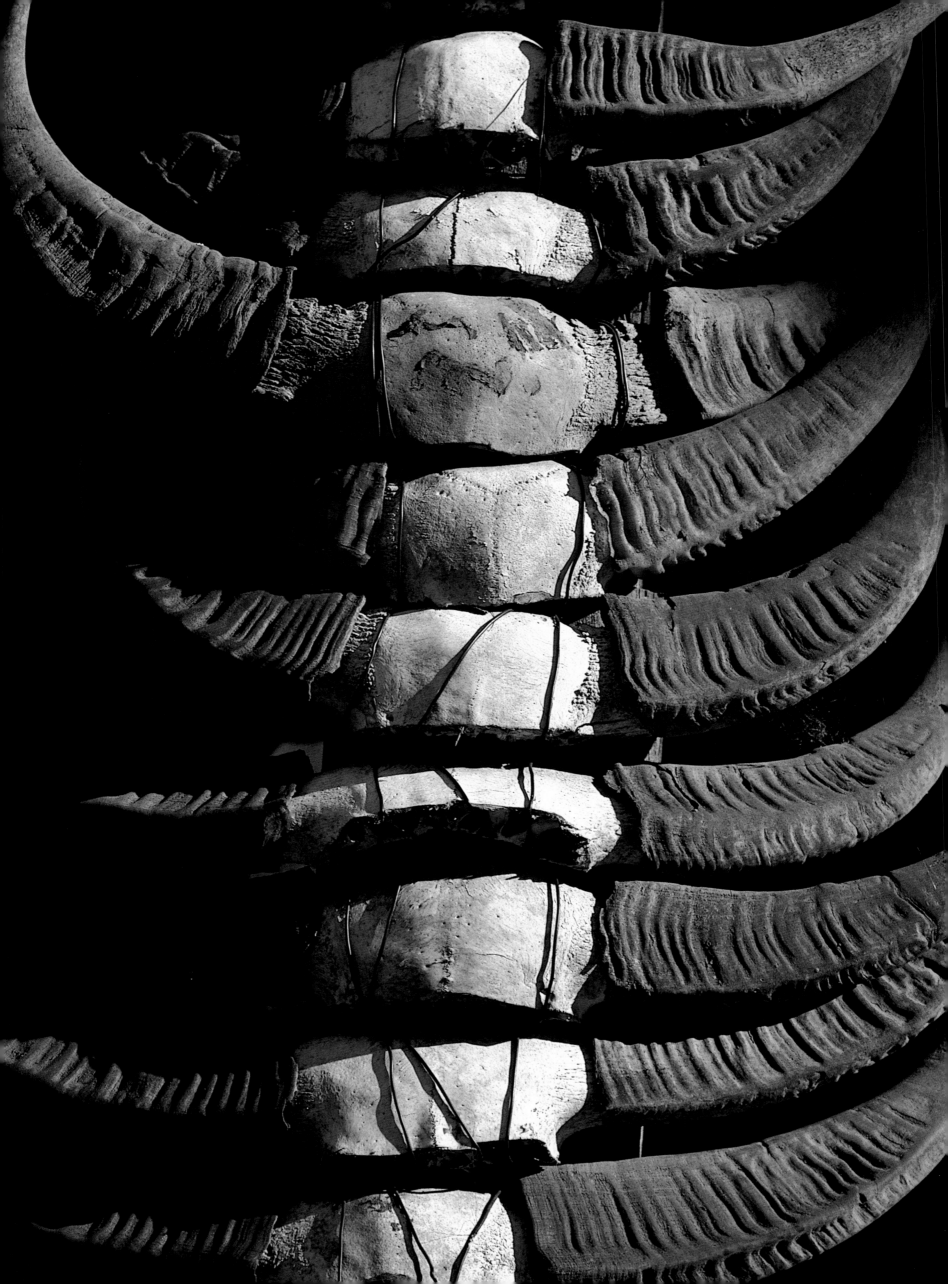

In Torajaland, the house is more than just a home: the traditional *tongkonan* dwellings are ancestral buildings, important for rituals and for prestige. Bold and dramatic – like so much of Toraja culture – these houses are among the area's oldest. Buffalo horns hung on their facades are a status symbol: a family's affluence and influence are measured by the size and number of horns.

Dominic Sansoni,
Sri Lanka

No sacrifice is too great, no task too arduous when it comes to commemorating the death of a revered relative or neighbor. Tradition still guides Toraja funeral rites – even when it means scaling the sheer face of a limestone escarpment. Tanah Toraja is Sulawesi's highland bastion of awesome rituals, and here the higher the status of the deceased, the higher the burial cave on the cliff wall, making for a harder climb on a bamboo stairway to heaven. **Dominic Sansoni,** *Sri Lanka*

The culture of the Bataks – who live in the highlands of North Sumatra – is expressed through a vigorous art and architecture *(right)*. Here the funerals of important people usually have two phases, each marking a different part of the deceased's spiritual journey. Invited guests bring food to the feast – like these women who came bearing baskets of rice *(left)*. **Eddy Posthuma de Boers,** *Netherlands*

I rian Jaya is the Indonesian half of New Guinea – a huge island with a landscape that ranges from glacier-edged mountains to trackless miles of coastal swamps. Irian Jaya is rich in minerals and resources, but developing the island is a great challenge: its diverse peoples have lived for centuries in isolation. Bringing them into the mainstream of development – the job of this government worker addressing a meeting *(left)* – is not an easy task.

Bruno Barbey, *France*
Robin Moyer, *USA*

A different ideal of beauty lies behind the dress and adornment of some women in Irian Jaya *(left)*. Unlike its counterpart elsewhere the Dani version of a mud bath carries solemn connotations: the mud is sometimes worn as a shroud of mourning. A Dani man carries the shopping home *(right)* from a market near Wamena. Other Dani men pose for formal portraits *(overleaf)*. Asmat warriors *(further overleaf)* put on a fierce front as they skillfully paddle out from their village on the Casuarina Coast. But fear not: These days it is just a welcome for visitors to their swampy home-lands on Irian Jaya's southern coast.

Robin Moyer (4), *USA*
Bruno Barbey, *France*

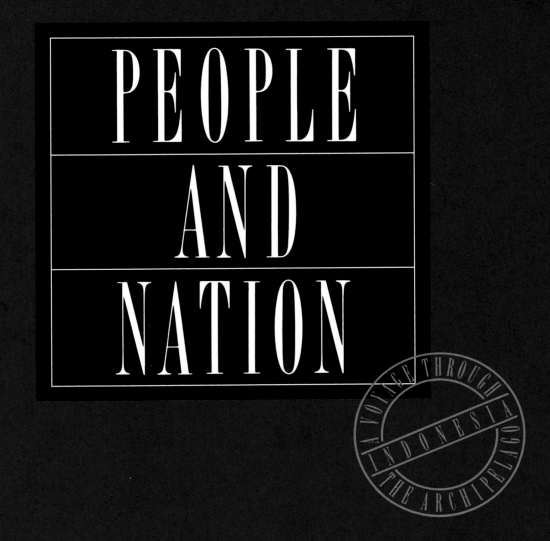

PEOPLE AND NATION

A VOYAGE THROUGH THE ARCHIPELAGO INDONESIA

I t was on the narrow mountain road on the way down from the Dieng Plateau that the accident occurred: a large fertilizer truck spilled its contents and tipped over, fast causing a pile-up of traffic on either side. This being Java, with more people per square kilometre than India, a crowd formed instantly. When the truck driver managed to wriggle out of the window obviously unhurt, there was laughter of relief. Then, imperceptibly, and without anyone overtly taking charge, a small miracle occurred: shovels were produced out of nowhere and some of the crowd began spooning the spilt fertilizer off the road. Three lengths of tough metal cord were attached to the side of the truck, volunteers organized themselves into tug-of-war teams, and a fourth cord was secured to the most powerful truck on the far side of the road. Everyone pulled, the overturned truck gave a lurch and then righted itself with a crash, settling on its four wheels. Soon the road was passable again.

It had been a very mixed crowd, with wealthy car owners alongside bone-poor peasants and laborers. Some of the faces were unmistakably Javanese, others Indian or Melanesian-looking. The truly astonishing thing had been its mood: no scenes, no fuss, no shouting, no recriminations. Nobody had made a show of knowing better than anyone else what to do. The incident recalled an earlier trip to Sunda Kelapa, Jakarta's harbor. In steaming heat, thousands of cars, trucks, handcarts and motorcycle rickshaws were trapped in an inextricable jam for over an hour. Anywhere else in the world there would have been a cacophony of tooting horns, tempers fraying and blood pressures soaring. Instead, being Indonesians, the drivers smiled and cracked jokes. Extreme patience and consensus behavior of almost unbelievable sophistication seemed to me the lessons to be learned from these incidents. Yes, an Indonesian friend concurred, but had a child been killed by the falling truck, the driver might well have been stoned to death. Violence, he added, like the boiling water beneath the chalky volcanic surface of the Dieng Plateau evident only in columns of hissing steam, is never far away.

I had seen a facet of Indonesian life and an instinctive response to a minor calamity that was only exceptional because such altruistic behavior had become so unusual in the West. "Here," as one Bali expatriate pointed out, "people rally when you're in trouble, and there's no question of ulterior motive, except possibly that they hope other people will rally when they need help. And if people have nothing else to give, they'll give their time." The blinkered 'turn-a-blind-eye' attitude that has become the Westerner's defense and survival mechanism in the alienating and often violent environment of the city, where every passerby is regarded either as a potential mugger or a conman, is still profoundly shocking to most Indonesians. What I had witnessed seemed the enactment in everyday life of the famous 'Pancasila' principles: these are based on values of unity, tolerance and consensus and were fostered with the clear aim of overcoming Indonesia's

Nation-building is more than a convenient catch-phrase for Indonesian politicians: it is an imperative for a sprawling archipelago of such incredible diversity. Through education and development Indonesia has found a balance between unity and expression of regional and cultural diversity. These students of a Chinese school in Jakarta *(preceding)* are witness to that process. **Leong Ka Tai,** *Hong Kong*

immense problems — economic, social, linguistic, and ethnic — as it faced independence.

Indonesia's entrance into the twentieth century was a rough one. The Dutch had never really tried to develop Indonesia, even as a potentially huge market for their goods. The colonials were content to appropriate wealth as speedily and efficiently as possible. Under the pressure of liberal forces at home, reforms were introduced to soften the rigorous demands of colonial rule, but the new policies often did more harm than good, at least initially, as private Dutch companies rushed in to fill the gap. In Java companies dealt with each village as a unit, and while this meant that traditional life was not greatly disrupted, it also meant that the farmer was isolated from the modernization going on around him.

The great boom of the early part of the century did little to modernize Indonesia. There was a vast expansion of plantations growing tobacco, rubber, tea, cane and coffee, in Sumatra and elsewhere. But plantation workers were often migrants from the overcrowded village of Java, and the huge commodity profits were rarely if ever reinvested in Indonesia. It was in the 1920s, stimulated by reforms and the possibilities of change glimpsed in the sympathies of some liberal Dutch, that Soekarno and other nationalists began to take early steps towards the struggle for independence. Reform Islam was a powerful force for change at this time also; Islamic schools were founded all across the country, teaching a creed that combined nationalism, faith, and a drive to modernize.

One of the great challenges facing the nationalists was to identify the forces, the ideas, and the symbols that would bind Indonesians together, that could unite them through the difficult struggles ahead. In particular the national language, Bahasa Indonesia, already proclaimed in 1928, played an intensive role in unifying the nation. By the time Soekarno became Indonesia's first President — and father figure — he was able to confirm Bahasa Indonesia as the official language of the new Republic. There were no

Banda Aceh, Aceh: The study of the Koran and its dictates for living is important here in one of the most devout enclaves of Islam in the archipelago. **Abbas,** *France*

language riots in reaction, no political movements in favor of more literary, local languages, as had occurred in India. Pancasila principles held the nation together and enabled the long-suffering Indonesian population to cope with the traumatic aftermath of the Japanese Occupation and a war of independence, including the tragic decline into irresponsibility of its charismatic leader many years later.

However varied ethnically, Indonesians share a number of characteristics. Though Sumatrans and Sulawesis are more forthright than the notoriously shy and secretive Javanese, certain patterns of behavior are common to all, among them a quiet dignity, a reluctance to project oneself, a philosophy of life marked by a certain fatalism, a refusal to attach too much importance to material things, and a tendency also to conceal one's real thoughts and feelings from the public's gaze. Yet Soekarno, Indonesia's great nationalist hero, was an example of all that was atypical of his people: utterly frank about himself and his private life, boisterous, outgoing, speaking his mind about any subject under the sun, Soekarno became the most famous Indonesian of the forties, fifties and sixties. His spellbinding oratory could turn hostile groups into fanatical devotees, setbacks into assets, failures into victories.

Medan, North Sumatra: Marble floors and columns mark the blend of Italian design and Moorish lines in the Grand Mosque. **Eddy Posthuma de Boers,** *Netherlands*

Soekarno and his peers had been among the first of the 'modern nationalists' committed to fighting for an end to colonialism and total independence since as far back as 1924. They had steered the country through the Japanese Occupation years with consummate skill, ostensibly cooperating with the invaders (Soekarno even accepting a Japanese medal and paying a little publicized trip to Japan in 1943, where he met Emperor Hirohito) while avoiding the stigma of collaboration.

On August 17, 1945, Soekarno and Hatta proclaimed 'total independence' for Indonesia. Four years of internal war followed, first against the British, who landed in Sumatra and Java to disarm the Japanese and stayed on to fight a 'holding operation' on behalf of the Dutch, who then took over and intensified the conflict. The Dutch did not manage to lay their hands on Soekarno, who eventually eluded them by moving to Yogyakarta, already an autonomous province under its enlightened, independence-minded sultan. Their stubborn resistance to change prolonged the fighting for at least two needless years. Only a United Nations move brought both sides to a conference table. Once independence had been proclaimed, Soekarno was ready to let bygones be bygones, establishing — at least at first — cordial relations with the erstwhile ruling power.

The Army, the Tentara Nasional Indonesia, emerging from its guerilla force status during the years 1945-49, saw him as the incarnation of its hopes and Soekarno in turn invested the military with a special importance, as an institution essential for nation-building. The Dutch claimed they had handed over a disparate collection of islands and races — and that there was no such thing as an Indonesian nation. To some extent this was true: such unity as existed at the time of independence had been against the ex-colonial power.

Soekarno held together this collection of islands as a nation. It was not easy. There were regional insurrections in Sumatra and the Moluccas. Agrarian communists flexed their muscles in a short-lived but bitter revolt in Madiun in East Java. The task of keeping it all together seems even more remarkable at a time when the world's superpowers still had recourse to a 'divide and rule' policy to try and keep their former colonies in line. Indonesian nationalism, once unleashed, was a powerful counterbalance against superpower politics in the region. Soekarno, because of his intuitive understanding of history (and also, perhaps, because of his mammoth ego) found a third way through the cold-war minefield of the fifties. At Bandung, a pleasant Javanese highland city which hosted the first Afro-Asia Conference, the 'Third World' was born, and Soekarno was its midwife. Almost overnight he became a media superstar, on a par with Tito, Nasser, and Nehru. He dramatized to the world the situation faced by Indonesia, as by Egypt and India, of an ancient civilization facing immense problems of poverty and development.

Soekarno, the Third World's most visible personality, displayed the showmanship of a truly great actor, the inspirational imagination of the prophet and the iron will of the dedicated politician. But his fantastic charisma was not enough to overcome grave economic problems. Expensive showy projects — steel mills, lavish conference centres, state-of-the-art stadiums — were not a substitute for the hard grass-roots efforts needed to bring meaningful development to the country. At the start of the sixties, the only plant running full time in Indonesia was the Government Mint, printing more and more devalued rupiah.

"Living dangerously," Soekarno said, "gives me the sense of an eagle." In the sixties it was Indonesia itself which teetered on the brink of disaster. Soekarno needed all of his vast skills to keep his balance on his eyrie at the top. On the ground, the political situation was becoming more and more polarized. Inflation reached outstanding proportions. There were errors of judgement that no amount of fiery oratory could conceal. Soekarno turned brutally against India for failing to support his quarrel with the Malaysian Federation and involved Indonesia in a state of war with Britain over the future of Borneo in the formation of the Federation; he turned against his military commander Nasution, whom he fired in 1962, and while his generals, among them a

Blambangan Pagar, Lampung, South Sumatra: The wide open gates of an old wooden home symbolize the genuine hospitality of the Indonesians.
Mahendra Sinh, *India*

veteran of the independence war named Suharto, loyally carried out their leader's commands, he raised a paramilitary force of 'young communists', giving them a privileged and completely undeserved status. Soekarno began to act erratically and came to rely more and more on NASAKOM, a coalition of groups supportive of him, but dominated by the powerful PKI, the Indonesian Communist Party, then the third largest in the world. Indonesia moved ever closer to the Asian communist 'hard core' nations of China, North Korea and Vietnam.

There had to be a breaking point. It came after a failed communist coup, which began with the brutal torture and murder of six leading officers of the Army's General Staff known for their anti-communist allegiances. After the initial confusion, the army, and the people, turned on the communists with all the fury of medieval times. There were many deaths, and inevitably, old scores were paid off in the course of the killings that had little to do with ideologies.

Java Sea, somewhere between Surabaya and Ujung Padang: Trimming the sails while at sea demands a steady foot as well as a firm hand.
Bernard Hermann, *France*

The odd thing about these years is that, though they marked a turning point in Indonesia's history, they are so seldom referred to today. Even in villages where the PKI had been strongest, and the violence had been greatest, memories are vague. Those who have lived through these events appear to regard them as a natural calamity, on a par with an earthquake or a volcanic eruption. And even among the country's most sophisticated economists, the mega-inflation years (1966-67), when a skilled surgeon's monthly salary was in real terms around 60 US cents, seem infinitely remote. The death toll became a frontpage story worldwide and condemnation was widespread throughout both Eastern and Western blocks. What outsiders failed to understand was that an exhausted, hungry and terrified population took the law into its own hands only after months of widespread Communist provocations. The violence, in the eyes of those who took part in it, had been essential to establish political stability as soon as possible.

These years, and their lingering legacy, will remain obscure to outsiders for many years to come. Is the strength of Pancasila ideology, as well as the remarkable political continuity Indonesia has enjoyed since the end of the sixties, a recognition of the costs of the chaos that resulted from the breakdown of order? Speculation is difficult here, but what we do know is that Indonesia passed over a watershed in the late sixties. The Army emerged from the crisis dominant and renewed, with a greater sense of mission as well as greater scope to bring about its goals of nation-building. We now know that many senior officers wanted Soekarno to be put on trial and that Suharto successfully prevailed to allow him to retire gracefully after an uneasy two years in which he and Soekarno remained co-presidents, a state of affairs unthinkable anywhere but in the land of Pancasila. I recall an evening at the residence of the then French Ambassador Claude Cheysson in July 1967, to which both Soekarno and Suharto were invited and had chosen to attend. Soekarno, who knows by this time his political career is virtually over, is full of banter, chortling at his own insensitive jokes. Suharto looks on, silent and disapproving, and yet as unwilling to stem Soekarno's embarrassing chatter as he was to remove him from public life. The spectacle of the two men comes to mind every time I land at Jakarta's new international Soekarno-Hatta airport for even in death Soekarno has been spared any loss of face. Unlike in other countries, and almost certainly because of an innate Indonesian respect for tradition, religion and continuity, the Republic has been unwilling to shatter what it once adored.

Keeping fit is a national passion, one certainly embodied in this monument of a mightily muscled man breaking his chains *(right)*. The Jakarta statue commemorates the liberation of Irian Jaya from Dutch rule. Fists and feet become a bruising ballet in the Indonesian martial art of *silat.* This group from the Presidential Guard practices *silat (overleaf)* as a kind of spiritual and mental discipline as well as a means of combat that incorporates the grace and rigorous precision of Javanese dance.
Paul Chesley, *USA*
G. A. Rossi, *Italy*

Sea covers more than three-quarters of Indonesia's five million square kilometers so the excellent reputation of its crack navy is to be expected. Unexpected are the seamanship and old-fashioned spit and polish on display at the Surabaya Naval Academy. Volatile Mount Merapi, literally "Fire Mountain", smoulders over Central Java, stealing some of the thunder *(overleaf)* from a formation of Republic of Indonesia Air Force jet fighters.
René Burri, *Switzerland*
G. A. Rossi, *Italy*

Only a drill, but with all the drama and daring of the real thing: firemen test their rescue capabilities near Jakarta. The fire department and all of Jakarta's other essential urban services have to cope with a city that is growing at a tremendous rate. Preparing for the possibility of a different kind of fire, a crack squad of red berets leap from a chopper in the sort of harrowing exercise *(preceding)* demanded of soldiers who must defend a vast archipelago of immense jungles, rugged mountains and other treacherous terrain. **Kartono Riyadi** (2), *Indonesia*
René Burri, *Switzerland*

Competitive marching in precision drills through the wide modern streets of Jakarta is a Sunday morning ritual. And like the more traditional rituals that occur everywhere in the archipelago, the Indonesians even manage to turn this into a spectacle of color and movement. Another element is music: it almost always fills the Indonesian air. On this mellifluous morning in Semarang *(overleaf)* a melodion band from a local high school marches to City Hall, adding a rousing rhythmic lilt to the cacaphony of the morning hustle and bustle.

Paul Chesley, *USA*
Hiroshi Suga, *Japan*

Shoulders straight; heels together, ladies. Pssst, that's heels together, young man! Young man? Well, the annual women's day at Jakarta's police academy often becomes more of a family affair, as do most events in Indonesia.
Paul Chesley, *USA*

I ndonesia's longtime President, and one of Asia's senior statesmen, President Suharto rules with a low-key and understated style. The son of Javanese farmers, Suharto is known to pay particular attention to agriculture and the rural development so crucial to Indonesia's future prosperity. Here the President consults with the Armed Forces Chief-of-Staff Gen. Tri Sutrisno at an armed forces function *(left)*. Together with his wife Ibu Tien and various ministers including Foreign Minister Ali Alatas, the President meets members of the press on his return flight to Jakarta *(bottom right)* after his historic Moscow meeting *(top right)* with the Soviet leader Gorbachov. **Beck Tohir,** *Indonesia*

Bhinneka
Tunggal Ika – Unity in
Diversity – is the creed
that Indonesia's
President Suharto and
the Golkar government
party rule under: A big
signboard in Jakarta
makes no doubt about
that. The slogan and
the Pancasila
ideology have
provided a rallying call
to which march
Indonesians of all
ethnic groups in all
walks of life.
Paul Chesley, *USA*

ducation and training are imperatives for a country as young and as quickly-changing as Indonesia. At the Theravada Buddhist monastery at the Candi Mendut near Central Java's Borobudur monument *(left),* a monk keys in computer data. In the highland city of Bandung students study in a language lab at Budi Utomo High School and future pilots get pointers at a flying school *(right).*
Ping Amranand,
Thailand
Agus Leonardus,
Indonesia

Whoops! Did someone turn out the lights? Fussing with the intricacies of traditional dress is a part of growing up in Indonesia *(right)*. Many of the millions of Indonesia's schoolchildren in classrooms from Sumatra to the Maluku far to the east *(left)* wear uniforms in the national colors, red and white.
Fendi Siregar, *Indonesia*
Wendy Chan, *Singapore*

All aboard! Java's excellent train system is a great way to see the island. Java has express trains that roar between Jakarta and Yoygakarta and along the north coast between Jakarta and Surabaya, smaller feeder lines, and a few very small guage railways which served the sugar cane plantations. While moving more than 100 million people along the rails can create a little bit of a crowd from time to time, the mood seems to be always a good one, and the smiles bid the traveler a good journey.

Steve Vidler, *UK*

and-some wooden Bugis schooners, many still handcrafted in the traditional way without nails, sail in and out of Indonesia's ports – on romantic airs. Bugis schooners, the ancient walls of the city and the minarets and domes of mosque impart a medieval look *(overleaf)* to South Sulawesi's bustling port and capital, Ujung Pandang. Indeed, the city still exhibits many vestiges of the 16th century when it was known the world over as Macassar, maritime center of the Dutch East Indies.

G Pinkhassov, *USSR*
Bernard Hermann, *France*

For South Sulawesi's handsome Bugis people home is usually where the next port is; these seafarers have settled in coastal villages on many islands. Two Bugis women *(left)* peer from a doorway in their sailing culture's historical home base, Ujung Pandang. Several hundred nautical miles south in Surabaya, Java's flagship port city, a man tests his strength and sense of balance *(right)* while loading cargo aboard a Bugis schooner. Once aboard it is time to secure the cargo *(overleaf)*. This crew is preparing for the next sail while in port at Surabaya.
Bernard Hermann,
France

Jakarta in the sixties was both an uncomfortable and an extremely incongruous place: not so much a town as a series of vaguely linked shantytown villages (*kampongs*), interspersed with towering statues, pillars, monuments and other, often abandoned attempts at grandeur. There were few traffic lights, a chaotic road network, and the usual 'stigmata' of Third World capitals: wrecked vehicles of a bygone age held together by string and the incredible skills of Indonesian mechanics; money-changers at every crossing; a marked absence of modern office blocks or hotels, except for the famous Indonesia. The traffic jams are practically all that's left of the bad old days, and now jalopies are few and far between. The communal taxi-buses, or *bemos*, are more likely to be stuck between brand-new minibuses, air-conditioned taxis imported from Japan and the latest BMWs with smoked-glass windows — a status symbol that is likely to disappear if the government ever carries out its plans to control congestion by allowing only cars with a full complement of passengers on Jakarta's streets during peak hours. Smoked glass would be a definite hindrance to police checks.

Another new incongruity is the prevalence of huge glass and concrete skyscrapers, ultra-modern banks and, inevitably, the omnipresent neon logos of Japanese cars, computers and electronic gadgets. Present-day Jakarta is a cross between Honolulu, downtown Miami and Osaka, with a few — very few — touches of local color: urchin street vendors selling everything from snacks and bottled water to gossip magazines; stalls dispensing Chinese noodles and snacks, the pungent *masakan* Padang; the occasional fortune teller or street barber. There are hardly any beggars and what is most striking of all throughout Indonesia is the comparative absence of old people. Though now progressively under control, Indonesia's birthrate in the first two decades of independence was phenomenally high, in part because Soekarno believed that the bigger the population, the bigger the country. Evidently he had little time for birth control. A profusion of night restaurants, bars and clip-joint hostess clubs, many of them catering for the Japanese, have sprung up in several neighborhoods. Most of the tiny hole-in-the-wall eateries, which serve all kinds of delicious Indonesian food, are now relegated to the suburbs, or to the *kampongs*. In downtown Jakarta, land has become too valuable and rents prohibitively high. There are ring roads, cloverleaf access ramps, and even fee-paying freeways, but they have failed to keep pace with the huge growth in wheeled traffic of all kinds, or with the expansion of the city as a whole. There were under five million inhabitants in Jakarta in 1972. Now there are close on nine million, and by the year 2000 it is estimated that Jakarta will be a megalopolis of over fourteen million people. This is a conservative estimate, but one already terrifying to the city planners and water councils.

Not even Indonesia's strongest advocates would claim that Jakarta is an attractive city, though it has parks, museums and antique shops well worth visiting. Most tourists give it a wide berth, transiting through the new Soekarno-Hatta airport on their way to Bali,

The most visible sign of Indonesia's economic boom of the past few years, huge new office and commercial developments are springing up all over Jakarta, in the latest high-tech architectural styles *(preceding),* transforming the look of this dynamic city.
Rio Helmi, *Indonesia*

Lombok or Sulawesi without bothering to stop off in the capital. Yet its luxurious hotels are booked up months in advance, and twenty-five more are in construction. The reason is that Jakarta is the epicentre of an economic boom which is making Indonesia, according to the influential *Far Eastern Economic Review*, the country to watch and invest in over the next decade. The intense, never-ending Jakarta bustle reflects the new prosperity and vitality of a country on the move. The traffic is constant, people start work at dawn, and shops stay open till all hours. It is discernible in the hundreds of hole-in-the-wall photocopying services and fax machines, in the army of smart secretaries braving the humid heat in motorcycle rickshaws and *bemos*. In this respect, the pace of life in Jakarta shows that Indonesia is a country fast emerging. The consequences may not be aesthetically pleasing, nor has such frenzied activity improved the quality of life, and the pace is only slightly slower outside the capital. In Yogyakarta, the streets are narrower, the town still recognizable to those who visited it in the sixties or even earlier, in the last days of Dutch colonial rule, when the nationalists found a haven in the Sultanate there. Nowhere is the boom more visible than in parts of Bali. Denpasar, once the sleepy shanty capital of a sleepy island, has been transformed into a workshop, the powerhouse of an island 'enjoying' a tourist boom unprecedented anywhere in the world. Kuta Beach and its surrounding streets are colorful enough, thanks to the scantily dressed, raucous tourist fauna, but the overall impression is of a cross between the Costa del Sol and an open-air Pier Import store — an eyesore for those who remember the old days but evidence again of a modernizing Indonesia. The politeness of the Balinese, and their fondness for euphemisms of all kinds, are exemplified in Nusa Dua, where a catering school amidst the kitsch luxury hotels is named 'The Institute for Applied Hospitality'.

The new affluence and expectations have of course transformed the country: in Bali, only the most venerable old ladies still leave their houses with their breasts bare, almost

Bandung, Central Java: The soft lines, symmetry and gentle humor of traditional Javanese art are apparent in a recent sculpture by Nyoman Nuarta. **Gerald Gay,** *Singapore*

defiantly following a custom in abeyance among the young. Off the beaten track, it is still possible to catch a glimpse of young Balinese women, unselfconsciously washing themselves in mountain streams, but probably having just washed down their gleaming new Toyotas.

Only in relatively undiscovered parts will you catch a glimpse of the older, more leisurely Indonesia. In Padang, horse-drawn taxi-carriages still do a thriving business; in Balangnipa on the Sulawesi coast, craftsmen still build ocean-going sailboats, the 400-ton *pinisi* with high-jutting bows modelled on those of the sixth and seventh centuries. In Jakarta's Sunda Kelapa harbor, there is row upon row of these boats, bringing in thousands of tons of teak, and leaving for Sulawesi,

Sumatra and Kalimantan with every kind of cargo, from new Peugeots to cement and crates of pre-cooked noodles. Fully equipped, these boats cost $150,000 each, and assembling them in Sulawesi is a lucrative business still. The hospitable boat-builders will happily show you around their craft. For all the hustle and bustle of the harbor, theirs is a fairly leisurely life, for they rarely brave the traffic to venture into town, preferring to take it easy on deck for days at a time while stores are unloaded. The dockers carrying huge loads, as in Conrad's day, teeter barefoot along the gangway, which is nothing more than a length of rough-hewn wood. These days, of course, the *pinisi* are powered not by sail alone, but also by diesel engine.

Kopang, Lombok: Indonesia has changed tremendously in the lifetime of this Sasak man. But he seems to have taken it all in stride.
Mike Yamashita, *USA*

The chances are that these too will be locally made, as Indonesia has shifted in the last few years from an agricultural to an industrial base. Recognizing that oil reserves are finite and fast diminishing, the government would like oil revenues to be no more than 30% of the Indonesian GNP, as compared to 80% at the peak of the oil crisis. Engines and cars are manufactured in Indonesia, as are TV sets, electronic gadgets, and even light aircraft like the Nusantara 250 and the CN–235 which have both found markets in Spain and the USA. Indonesia's industrial potential is still on an upward curve, and liable to grow exponentially as wages in the rest of Southeast Asia continue to rise. It is becoming more practical to open a factory in Indonesia than it is to manufacture consumer goods in either Taiwan, South Korea or Singapore. And for all the new economic liberalism of the eighties and nineties, certain legislation still compels Indonesian entrepreneurs to become manufacturers and not just trading 'compradors'. The export of teak is restricted to encourage the manufacture of furniture, for example, and stringent import duties encourage the growth of local industry. There are plans to create a Shannon-type customs-free zone on the island of Batam, eventually to rival nearby Singapore.

How realistic and how broad-based is the Indonesian boom? Foreign bankers, local businessmen and economists believe that the only stumbling block is the scarcity of technologically-trained local management. Despite the leaps in education over the last forty-five years — it comes as a shock to realize that the illiteracy rate on the eve of Independence was over 80% — there will never be enough skilled Indonesian managers, engineers, lawyers or business school graduates. Some expatriates also feel that recent mergers and newly-formed conglomerates have concentrated new money in the hands of Chinese bankers and entrepreneurs, giving them clout far in excess of their numbers. These Chinese tycoons are far more Indonesian than previous generations, but for all that, says one banker, "the gifted Javanese business school graduate risks ending up as a high-level executive in a Chinese family conglomerate rather than heading his own firm". Government regulations try to guard against this through cooperatives and worker participation, but the business perks and risk-taking of the Chinese surpass those of all other Indonesian nationals. "There is still," says one foreign resident of Yogyakarta, "the feeling here that the old leisurely ways are worth preserving, and that means not working too hard and not busting a gut to acquire worldly goods simply because they are on display elsewhere."

Indonesia today pays its respects to the economic achievements of Japan. Despite the failure of their wartime 'Great East Asian Co-Prosperity Scheme', the Japanese have single-mindedly pushed themselves to the forefront of world markets. Some leading hotels bow to the supremacy of Japanese visitors, giving them, at their own request, a whole floor to themselves. As any hotel lobby shows, as well as the rapid proliferation of Japanese restaurants and sushi bars, the Japanese outnumber businessmen of any other nationality, and are treated by the Indonesians with the kind of respect American entrepreneurs elicited in the fifties.

Another notable change in modern-day Indonesia is the growing disparity between the overcrowded island of Java and the rest of the nation. In some parts of Java there are as many as two thousand people living on one square kilometer — a higher density of people than anywhere except Hong Kong. The government is therefore offering incentives to attract Javanese and Balinese to settle on the 'outer islands'. This has worked best in cases where small-scale entrepreneurs have, of their own volition, set up shop in Kalimantan and Sulawesi, and indeed the insularity of the past is giving way to freer relations between the islands. It is not unusual these days for an entrepreneur to have a father from Lombok, a mother from Kalimantan, to make his fortune in Bali and then invest part of it in a restaurant or boat-building yard in Sulawesi. Enforced resettlement, however, has been resisted, and more fortune-hunters are moving into

Solo, Central Java: Pencil tucked precariously in pocket and cap cocked forward, a scout snaps to a smart salute at a train station.
Steve Vidler, *UK*

Bali than moving out, and who indeed would ever willingly leave the paradise island? Islands like Kalimantan and Lombok are equally paradisical but require less passive economic policies and more directed investment to realize their potential in the tourist market. This raises another fundamental question, that of Indonesia's long-term political future.

Since the failure of the 1965 communist coup, and especially since Soekarno's death in 1970, the military have played a key role in running the country. Not that the Indonesian Republic is openly a military regime. Theirs is not a visible presence. There are fewer uniformed people on the streets than in many a so-called democracy, but everyone knows that key decisions are taken by men like President Suharto who have moved into government roles after a lifetime of military service. Early retirement for senior officers means that they can embark on a second civilian career as senior administrators, government officials, and even as bankers and businessmen.

The system has worked, in large part, because of the moral authority of the *bapak*, or father of the country: President Suharto himself. But things are changing rapidly, and sooner or later Indonesia will surely have to face the new problems posed by rapid expansion with a more broadly-based, democratic system. Badly burnt by the chaos engendered by an attempt at democracy, followed by a 'guided democracy' in the fifties and early sixties, the current leaders are reluctant to rock the boat, especially now that economic indicators show Indonesia in recovery and on the brink of a major breakthrough. President Suharto insists that he is not, as is the case in military regimes elsewhere, 'president for life'. But the highly influential military lobby, though divided on other policy matters, remains adamantly opposed to the return of what it derisively refers to as 'liberal democracy'. Perhaps the coming generation of Indonesians will have the answer. Standards of education are remarkably high, and the crowds of schoolchildren, smartly uniformed in even the remotest parts of the Republic, probably hold the key to the future. The role of the military and the army's share in the running of the country will almost certainly be adapted when they become decision-makers themselves.

Finally, there is the question of coming to terms with the new Indonesia without entirely giving up the old. Here the Indonesian psyche helps: Javanese and Balinese dances and temple rituals are completely independent of tourism, even though tourists flock to see them. Unlike certain parts of Africa where dances and rituals are consciously recreated for foreigners, Indonesian culture not only remains uppermost in people's lives, but keeps on evolving. In a remote Balinese village I recently watched a dance group rehearse their complicated steps and gestures. Their teacher turned out to have a Master's Degree in musicology from a well-known university in California where she had studied and taught for the last three years. Balinese dances, she insisted, were not rigidly patterned for all time. There was room for invention, for adaptation. The very fact that the complex gamelan sound is unwritten and improvized makes it music as contemporary as jazz and blues. Gamelan is very much akin to the soul of Indonesia itself. They share an emphasis on continuity, consensus, variety and tolerance, along with a capacity to develop, to adapt, and to endure. Above all they are unique, a country and art form unlike any other in the world.

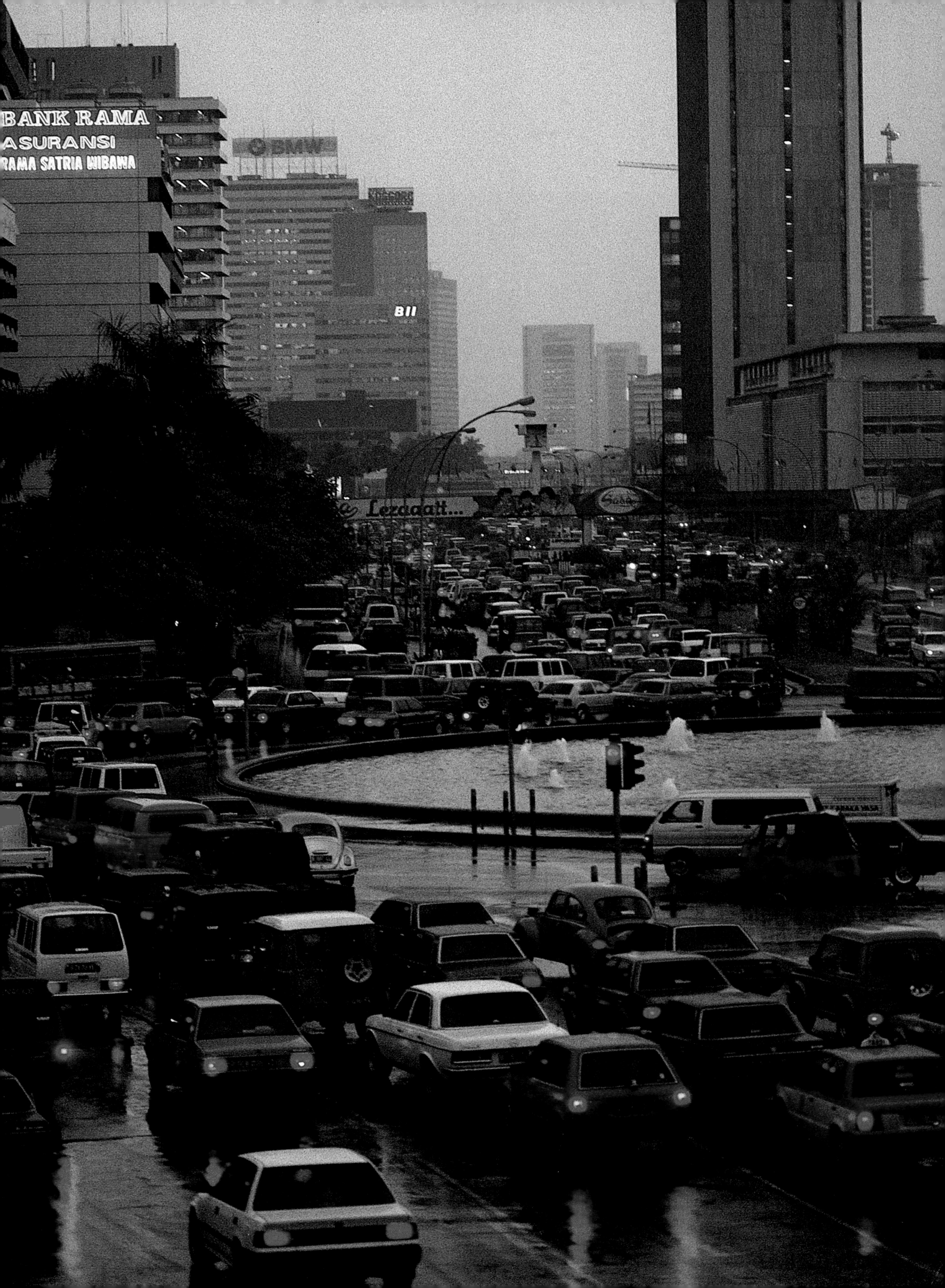
BANK RAMA
ASURANSI
RAMA SATRIA WIBAWA
BMW
BII
Lezaaatt...

A
sculptured flame
coated with 33
kilograms of gold gives
Monas, Indonesia's
national monument, a
kind of perpetual glow
that reflects the warm
inner spirit of the
country's people. The
137-meter marble spire
anchors Jakarta's
government district
amid a rising wall of
modern office towers.
It was built by
Indonesia's founding
father and first
president, Soekarno.
Rio Helmi, *Indonesia*

Befitting a vast nation with so many cultures, the Indonesians get around on great variety of vehicles. The three-wheeled, pedal-powered *becak* is popular in Yogyakarta *(top left)* but Jakarta traffic *(right)* is getting too fast and heavy for slower moving *becak:* City Hall wants them off the roads. Burgeoning traffic jams are the bain of rapidly industrializing countries like Indonesia – but a boon to its hustling young entrepreneurs *(bottom left)*.

Paul Chesley, *USA*
Richard Kalvar, *USA*
Bruno Barbey, *France*

It is a big job keeping Java's 100 million people employed. Labor-intensive enterprise is crucial for Indonesia's growing economy. This textile factory *(left)* in Bandung is part of an important export industry. The thriving *kretek* industry is also labor intensive – to say the least. Talk of automating the manufacture of the clove-flavored cigarettes falters in the face of reality: factories like this Gudang Garam facility *(right and overleaf)* in Kediri in north central Java provide jobs for 45,000 women.

Gerald Gay, *Singapore*
Richard Kalvar (2), *USA*

Lured by the prospects of a large – and happy – workforce, foreign multinationals from countries like Japan have invested heavily in Indonesia; the workers (*left*) at Astra Motors in Jakarta, for instance, assemble the Indonesia's Toyota Kijang – a vehicle especially designed for island roads – from transmission to tailpipe (*right*).

Fendi Siregar, *Indonesia*

Bandung, a pleasant city in Java's uplands, is a hub of technology with its high-flying aircraft industry. At the sprawling Industri Pesawat Terbang Nusantara, employees work on a propellor engine *(left)* and Bell 412 helicopters roll off an assembly line *(top right)*. An updated image for Indonesia's international airline Garuda Indonesia, has been engineered by its President Director Soeparno.
Fendi Siregar, *Indonesia*
Rio Helmi, *Indonesia*

I ndonesia's new elite: Businessmen have built their fortunes as Indonesia grows richer: people like Soedono Salim, (Liem Sioe Liong) one of the wealthiest men in the world *(top left)*, businessman and mega-property developer Ciputra *(left)*, and Sudwitakmono *(bottom center)* of Bogasari Flour Mills and related companies. Others have made their mark in government affairs, like Army Chief of Staff Tri Sutrisno *(top right)*, who has brought the military into new dialogues with other groups. There is another kind of elite: Guruh Soekarnoputra *(right)* is acclaimed as a composer and choreographer, Iwan Tirta *(center near right)* is a leading batik textile designer, Iwan Sagito *(bottom right)* is an artist whose Javanese surrealism is attracting international interest, and Christine Hakim *(top center)* is an award-winning actress whose films have been invited to Cannes and other festivals.

Mark Wexler (6), *USA*
Rio Helmi, *Indonesia*
Gerald Gay, *Singapore*

The *becak* continues to be popular form of transport in Indonesia's cities and towns: in Yogyakarta, they form a veritable army. *Becak* drivers, here seen at ease at a Yogya *becak* workshop *(left)*, personalize with paintings the vehicles they spend most of their waking hours pedaling *(right)*.
Hiroshi Suga, *Japan*
Bruno Barbey, *France*

A variety of spicy soups with lamb, chicken or beef constitute the menu painted on canvas at a *warung*, Indonesia's rough equivalent of a combination fast-food restaurant and local pub. Other streetside stalls and shops are *(clockwise from bottom left)* a tailor's shop, a teahouse, a cigarette seller's, a songbird shop and a provisioner's, who stocks an extra supply of soya- and chilly-based condiments for flavorful local cuisine. Indonesia's modern urban culture is as colorful and graphic as any of its traditional ones: Hand-painted movie billboards and advertising hoardings *(overleaf)* are a fixture in cities and towns, including Padang *(right),* Menado *(bottom left)* and Jakarta *(top left).*

Leong Ka Tai, *Hong Kong*
G Pinkhassov, *USSR*
Eddy Posthuma de Boers (2), *Netherlands*
Bruno Barbey, *France*
Star Black, *USA*
Basil Pao, *Hong Kong*
Mike Hosken, *New Zealand*
Paul Chesley, *USA*

238

I ndonesia is noted for exotic fruits like the durian, the snake-skinned *salak* and hairy *rambutan*. Not as exotic is the watermelon, which seems to have crossed cultures and palates the world over – including Lombok, where this watermelon man does a brisk business.

Mike Yamashita, *USA*

The Green Revolution, cheap fertilizer and improved roads and transport have meant that Indonesia's markets – especially in the more fertile islands of Sumatra, Bali, Java and Sulawesi – are full to overflowing with goods. This market stall in Java proudly displays a flavor-packed array of chillies, onions and other ingredients essential to Indonesian food. The chilly pepper was brought to Indonesia from the Americas by the Portuguese. It is now an integral part of Indonesia's varied cuisine.

Hiroshi Suga, *Japan*

Free enterprise flourishes in Indonesia, sometimes to the frustration of economic analysts trying to keep tabs on who is selling what to whom, and for what price. This sort of market economy requires a pair of strong shoulders, especially if you are carrying an unwieldly bunch of wooden shoes to the Sweta market in Lombok (top left) or sheaves of rice – each stalk cut individually with a tiny hand sickle – bound for a granary in West Java (bottom left) In one market a woman cooks *krupuk*, pungent prawn and flour crackers that come in some remarkably unlikely colors *(right)*.
Mike Yamashita, *USA*
P. van der Velde, *Netherlands*
Paul Chesley, *USA*

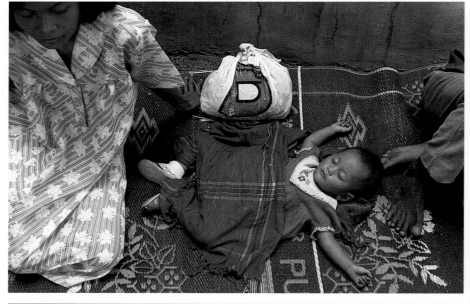

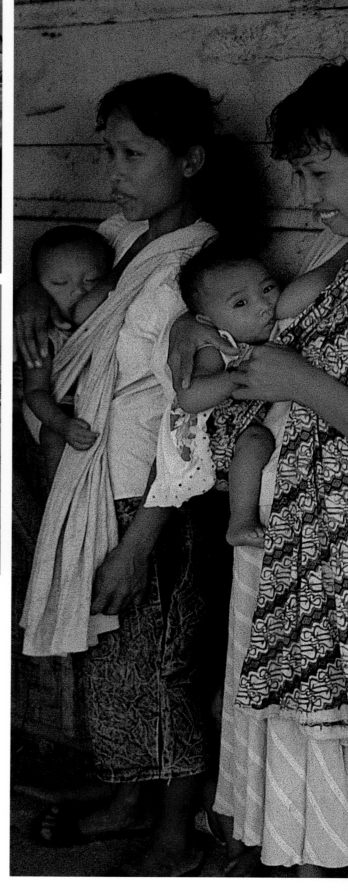

Mom's breast is best when baby is hungry; these healthy youngsters are ample evidence of that *(right)*. These beaming young women are in for a check-up and some infant care tips at a primary health centre in Bumi Sari, a village in Sumatra's Lampung province. Whether on the move at a Javanese train station *(above)* or in a ceremony to celebrate their 40th day in Kalimantan *(below)*, Indonesian children are especially treasured. "Oh, I'm just hanging around" *(preceding)* means exactly what it says when growing up in the islands. A sarong sling helps keep baby out of trouble when mom is busy at a marketplace in the South Kalimantan city of Palangkarya: snug under the chin but more comfortable than it looks.

Mahendra Sinh, *India*
Steve Vidler, *UK*
Leong Ka Tai, *Hong Kong*
Martin Kers, *Netherlands*

Caught in a cloudburst at a bus station in Jakarta? As the Indonesians say, *tidak apa-apa*: never mind, nothing to worry about. Not when there are enterprising youngsters around who are happy to keep you dry under one of their umbrellas – for a small tip
Paul Chesley, *USA*

Sweet, sweet coffee, tea, cigarettes and snacks while the spare hours away in coffeeshops and *warung* all over Indonesia, from Aceh *(right)* to Central Java *(left)* and points east. Keeping long nails is sometimes considered a sign that the wearer does not have to engage in manual labor: one young dandy takes this status symbol to extreme lengths *(top left)*. For many Indonesians, like this man lugging a load of bamboo tubes filled with fermented palm brew *(overleaf)*, manual labor is a proud way to earn a living.

Ian Berry, *UK*

G. Pinkhassov, *USSR*

René Burri, *Switzerland*

DIARY OF THE VOYAGE

A VOYAGE THROUGH INDONESIA THE ARCHIPELAGO

APRIL 1989 — AUGUST 1990

When producing a book of any importance – whether it's a pocket guide to a small island or a calf-bound volume about cut crystal – the first question a publisher will ask is "What about the numbers?" In most cases, such a bookmaker is asking about the actual costs involved to originate the book and produce it, that is, typeset text, color separate pictures, print, bind and ship the finished product.

These two basic publishing figures were also of first- consideration importance in the making of this particular title – *Indonesia: A Voyage Through the Archipelago* – but of equal significance were the dizzying logistics, or other numbers if you will, involved in attempting to produce the ultimate book ever produced about Indonesia. As a worldwide travel destination, Indonesia is a relative newcomer, at least partly because Indonesia is one of the most complex nations on earth. It includes within its multi-cultural, geographically diverse mileu some of the most inaccessible and fascinating land masses on this planet.

Given the above (and much, much more), the folks who produced this book had to spend countless meeting hours just deciding how to "cover" this country and give the reader-viewer a book that would somehow do the country editorial and pictorial justice. How, within the space of 288 pages and some 375 photographs (culled from more than 120,000 pictures taken by 45 fine photographers) would this be accomplished? What follows is a peek behind the shutters of the publishers, writers, photographers and other creative people and institutions who made this voyage possible.

July, 1988, Singapore

At this early time in the evolution of a book then Singapore-based publisher Didier Millet and his creative director, Leonard Lueras, had just returned from Thailand where they had joined forces with friends and colleagues to launch a book entitled *Thailand, Seven Days in the Kingdom*. The success of the Thai book attracted the attention of Joop Ave, Indonesia's innovative Director-General of Tourism, and during a meeting he had with Millet and Lueras, Ave inquired whether it would be possible to produce an equally beautiful book to commemorate Indonesia's 45th Anniversary of Independence in 1990. Ave explained that the number 45 was considered very auspicious because the proclamation of independence which in effect freed the country after nearly 400 years of colonial rule. " I would like to commemorate this anniversary with the finest book ever produced about my country," Ave said, and with that comment this book was "verbally" set into motion.

November 1988, Paris

Publisher Millet moved from Singapore to Paris and there established a new publishing house, Editions Didier Millet. From his office in the "city of light", Millet enlisted the support of two co-publishers, John Owen of San Francisco and Kevin Weldon of Sydney for a project code-named "Indonesia 1990". Faxes whizzed between Millet's Montparnasse office and Ave's Pariwisata office on Jakarta's Jln Kramat Raya. Finally in March 1989 Ave sent a brief telex to Millet asking if he, Owen and Weldon could rendezvous with him in Jakarta to initiate serious discussions regarding the book. At this meeting, Director-General Ave agreed to actively enlist commercial sector sponsors that would be crucial to finance the book and following handshakes around his desk, *Indonesia 1990* shifted into second publishing gear.

Early March, 1989, Sanur, Bali

Millet Weldon and Owen called for a first creative strategy meeting, which was held in the office of Image Network Indonesia in Sanur, Bali. In attendance at that meeting were Millet, Weldon and Owen, plus Lueras, Bali-based photographer Rio Helmi and Dawn Low, a Hong Kong-based associate of Owen's who was on a sabbatical leave as the Asia circulation director of the *International Herald Tribune*. At this brainstorming session the book's editorial approach was discussed, and it was agreed that Millet-Weldon-Owen would publish the book in cooperation with Director-General Ave, and that the key members of the creative team would be Low as Project Director, Lueras as

Creative Director and Helmi as Chief Photographer and Assignments Editor. Peter Schoppert, a Singapore-based publisher, was to be recruited as the books' Chief Editor.

Mid-April 1989, Jakarta

An important budgeting and organization meeting was held in Ave's Pariwisata board room to discuss the project with Ave's aides and representatives of Garuda Indonesia Airways and Foote, Cone, and Belding, the advertising agency which represents Pariwisata worldwide. At this meeting, Garuda, a crucial sponsor agreed in principle to support the project by providing the transport needed to ferry the many renowned photographers who would have to be flown from around the world to (and from) Indonesia to participate in the one-week long photo shoot once the project was officially underway.

Late April 1989, Bali

Following the meeting in Jakarta, creative work began in earnest. Following a series of spirited midday and late night meetings a working title for the book was agreed upon: *Indonesia: A Voyage Through the Archipelago*. At the end of the one particularly enthusiastic exchange of ideas, Australian publisher Weldon issued an on-on battle cry: "Let's go, Archipelago!", and the team like the sound of his impromptu charge so much that they immediately adopted it as the book projects' slogan. This slogan later appeared on T-shirts, baggage stickers and promotional materials, and proved so popular with the Indonesian government that it was adopted as the slogan for the 1991 "Visit Indonesia Year" international campaign.

Early May, 1989, Bali, Jakarta and Paris

For a few weeks after Weldon chanted "Let's Go!" the logistics and creative teams quietly began drafting more detailed plans of attack. Everybody knew (based on past experience in other countries) that they would have to proceed cautiously until more commercial sponsors joined the Voyage's bandwagon. Transport to and from Indonesia was more or less promised, and Ave was positively supportive and upbeat, but who, the team wondered, would underwrite expensive items such as films and processing (about 5000 rolls worth), or hotel room nights and meals for 45 photographers and an even larger support staff? Until those fiscal details could be spoken for, the book would have to remain in cautious check.

With Ave and Millet acting as diplomatic pointmen-salesmen, a number of conservative corporate executives were approached and within a surprisingly short time the project was joined by Kodak Films, the Jakarta Hilton International Hotel and, in Bali, the Nusa Dua Beach Hotel (managed by Indonesia's Aerowisata group of hotels). Much more funding would eventually be necessary, but once airfares, room and board and films were in the bag, the idealistic "Let's Go!" call to action became a businesslike "OK, let's go ahead".

Mid-May through Mid-July, 1989

Time was short, so in order to quickly set the various wheels, paddles and rotor blades of the project into motion, the Project Team split into three camps. In Bali, Lueras and Helmi ploughed ahead with research and preparation of assignment briefings. Helmi journeyed to remote parts of Indonesia to make initial contact and discuss plans with people who would later assist photographers as guides in remote regions such as Irian Jaya, the Maluku and Kalimantan.

In Jakarta, Low set up a project office in a suite at the Jakarta Hilton International Hotel, and from that big city headquarters began making daily sales calls to other potential sponsors. Low was soon joined in this effort by Seti-Arti Kailola, an Indonesian lady well versed in the intricacies of Indonesian boardroom behavior and financing. With the encouragement and support of Ave, Low and Kailola slowly but assuredly added more names to the roster of Voyage sponsors.

A complete press-time list of sponsors appears elsewhere in this book, but the following excerpts from an early project press release outline the role the initial project sponsors played in making the book possible:

"When the need arose to link the photographers' routes to connect with the Garuda flight schedule, the Project Team approached KLM Royal Dutch Airlines for assistance. KLM quickly responded with their pledge to participate ... Jim Wiryaman of PT Mantrust warmly applauded the project and President Tegoeh Soetantyo added his support (also) through PT Mantrust ... The backing from the Indonesian banking community was whole-hearted and the Project received much help from Bank Umum Nasional, Bank Duta, BDNI, Bank Bumi Daya and BNI ... representing the multi-trading corporations are Dharmala Group, Rajawali Group, Plaza Indonesia, Indobuildco, Keramik Diamond and Bakri Brothers ... To assist with their professional services and to account for the sponsors' cash contribution, Drs Siddharta & Siddharta / Coopers & Lybrand, the firm of Chartered Accountants, took on the massive task of being the Project Auditors and accountants. Commented Bob Williamson, Kodak's Manager in Indonesia, "We believe that Indonesia has much that lends itself to photography, and we are delighted to be a part of this very exciting commemorative book on Indonesia..."

In Paris meanwhile, Millet and his staff started issuing invitations to the various well-known photographers he and the Project Team hoped would join the week-long shoot in far-away Indonesia. Fax machines bleeped and hummed in the world's major cities (and even in remote towns and villages) and very soon answers started pouring into the Paris office. The response to the invitations was almost unanimous, "Yes, I'm coming. Agreement follows", and within a few weeks of sending out the all-points bulletins, the Project Team had recruited the services of a veritable "who's who of Photography". When a final list of photographers was drawn up, it was noted, ironically, that they represented 19 different countries. Given the uncanny coincidence of 19 countries and 45 photographers (who will be working on a book to be published in honor of the year 1945), the numerologically inclined members of the Project Team proceeded to work with new vigor and the feeling that good luck was on their side.

Mid-July through mid-August

The project team expanded its ranks by recruiting the professional services

of a number of important staff members. Among these were Anne Greensall, who arrived in early August, and from her room at the Jakarta Hilton began liaising with Garuda, KLM and other sub-carriers to make arrangements for travel for photographers and staff members. Multi-lingual Halida Ilahunde Leclerc was hired as project coordinator in charge of public relations; Amna S Kusumo took over the post of research and logistics coordination working closely with Helmi. From Ave's Pariwisata offices came a government relations team led by Azhari Abdullah, Tjetjep Suparman, Sri Juniarti and Peter Pangaribuan. These new staffers and members of the project team criss-crossed Jakarta by day, held informal planning meetings at night, and feverishly made the thousand-and-one preparations that would be required to service staff, photographers and sponsoring agencies once the big August-September shoot week began.

18 August 1989, Jakarta

In mid-August Millet and Owen proceeded to

Jakarta to hold a 18th August press conference at Pariwisata during which the Voyage was officially announced and made public. Ave introduced members of the Project Team to the press, and said "A book project of this magnitude with the aim of capturing Indonesia's dizzying diversity of people, culture, landscape and its harmonious integration within one society is every publisher's dream. To see Indonesia through the eyes of 45 very individualistic photographers from around the world gives this book an interpretation that is extremely

exhilirating." Owen announced that the publishers were planning on bringing out over 50,000 copies in several languages for worldwide distribution. That evening on national television, and the next day in the print media, the people of Indonesia became aware of the Indonesia '90 Book Project for the first time. The Project Team began counting down and with extreme urgency.

Mid-August, Jakarta

The entire Voyage book project team gathered at the Jakarta Hilton Hotel, commandeered three adjoining suites as a headquarters office and communications center, and began final shoot week scheduling. This headquarters, early on referred to as the Nerve Center, (and later the Nervous Center) hummed and rattled with activity during the ten days prior to shoot week. The Project Team enlisted a team of cultural researchers from Etnodata, a research and publishing group to back up Helmi and Kusumo with nationwide ethnographic and geographical

input – crucial once the photographers were sent out on complex assignments. Also on hand were top reservations and public relations staff from Garuda, plus a number of people from Setia Tours, the group being contracted to provide guides, translators and local transport.

the 23rd, 24th, 25th of August, 1989, Jakarta

With new staff members and Project Team leaders in place, all shoot week systems were go, and on the above three dates, both foreign and Indonesian photographers began arriving from their home ports alone and in small groups. The invitees were met and garlanded upon arrival at Jakarta's Soekarno-Hatta airport. As the photographers set foot in Indonesia they were escorted to a waiting bus and immediately shuttled to their weekend home at the Jakarta Hilton.

Friday 25 August, Sunda Kelapa Harbor, Jakarta

Most of the photographers were now physically in Indonesia, so it was time to celebrate their arrival. As an opening ploy, the Project Team commissioned the services of an extra-big Bugis schooner, and just after twilight staff members, photographers and invited guests were bussed to Jakarta's historic Sunda Kelapa Harbor on the Strait of Java, This is the home of the world's last great working sailboat fleet, and a big Welcome to Indonesia party began on board the Voyage's host schooner as the craft put to sea. It was an appropriate way for staff and photographers to get acquainted, shake off jet lag, and prepare for a more complex Voyage through the Archipelago which awaited everybody during the week to come.

Saturday, 26 August, 1989

After a wake-up breakfast in the rooms, the photographers and Project Team staffers repaired to a Hilton conference room where they sat cross-legged on mats and participated in a traditional Javanese *selamatan* ceremony replete with the

cutting up of special rice pyramids and the drinking of aromatic teas. Following the ceremonies, blessing the project, the photographers were introduced to the media by Director General Ave. Afterwards the photographers went for a lunch with a group of Indonesia's Generation of '45, veterans of Indonesia's revolution, who had some wise words to say on the significance of the year's celebrations.

Sunday, 27 August

Very early this morning, the photographers and invited Project Team members regrouped in a side-lobby at the Hilton, and after checking by security officers they boarded two buses bound for Tapos, an experimental livestock ranch maintained by Indonesia's President Suharto. After about an hour and a half of travel, the two busloads of Voyagers emerged to find President Suharto himself standing there greeting them with a broad smile and a rare Presidential handshake. This scene was punctuated by the staccatto clicks of 45 professionally-operated cameras, especially so when a Project Team member presented

Suharto with a *wayang kulit* puppet decked out in a camera vest and two *wayang kulit* cameras. Suharto officially welcomed the photographers and gave them his thoughts on Indonesia's development, then took them all on a casual walking tour of his Tapos ranch. He later invited everybody to have lunch at the nearby Presidential Istana (or palace) in Bogor. The two-bus entourage proceeded to the Bogor Istana, where they enjoyed a formal luncheon and were entertained by an assortment of dancers, and musicians.

The real highlight of the day's unexpected audience with President Suharto came at the end of the walking tour at Tapos. Before saying Selamat Jalan to the photographers, the President posed with them for the group's first formal photograph. President Suharto them took up a camera himself, and took a picture of his famous photo-world guests. In all, the Voyagers spent nearly three hours with Indonesia's leader.

Later that evening, following their return to Jakarta from Bogor, the Voyagers were greeted by Kodak at a cocktail party in the Hilton's executive club, and then walked to the Batak Village on the spacious grounds where they enjoyed a local feast, and were warned to get some rest in anticipation of the week's shooting assignments which were to begin the following morning.

Monday, 28th August, 1989

As dawn rose, and the photographers began hopping on airplanes and other vehicles bound for all parts of the Archipelago, the photographers were generally on their own. Some had guides and translators, but most did what they usually do on assignment – that is winged it – trusted their instincts to where they would get the best light and the best pictures. The Headquarters Office was still kept busy with last-minute logistic matters. When for example Magnum photographer René Burri was having trouble obtaining proper clearances to shoot the Indonesian Army in combat exercises, he and Helmi paid a call on General Tri Sutrisno, the Indonesian Armed Forces Chief of Staff. Gen Tri was well aware of the project, so he simply gave orders into coded phones on his desk, and within a very short time a ranger unit of the Army was in full combat gear – complete with

David Bowie

Mr. René Burri,
Wegackerstrasse 7,
8041 Zurich.

Dear René,

Here, nearly reluctantly, are my submissions as requested.
Most of the choices are those of Mr. Favrod, however, I
also included three of mine.

I suspect I need not mention that these negs are very
personal to me and I leave them entirely in your care.
All I ask is that you return them to me whenever
convenient.

I do hope we cross paths again on our mutual globe-
trotting, and I hope one of my holiday snaps is good
enough to join the work of such a distinguished team
of artists.

Best regards,

facepaint and zany camouflage – and ready to engage in helicopter assault exercise for Burri. Later, when veteran pilot and photographer Guido Rossi of Italy had problems arranging with the Air Force for a ride in a fighter plane, a few more calls quickly took care of that problem. Fighter planes were rolled out for Rossi, he was given his pick of the lot, and later found himself flying by Central Javanese volcanos at supersonic speed. Like Burri and Rossi, the rest of the photographers were on target and

firing away, and during the next seven days the Indonesian archipelago was captured on film like never before.

Sunday, 3 September, Bali

Bruno Barbey stumbled up to the registration counter with some 250 extra kilograms of luggage. *"Souvenirs de guerre"* he joked, explaining that he had brought back some amazing Asmat artifacts. "The pictures are good too, he laughed. India's Mahendra Sinh, didn't think it was too funny. He and a guide were stopped on a remote road in Sumatra and held up by a renegade group of Kubu tribesmen. "They didn't want anything valuable; they just wanted whatever food we had with us", he said. American Mark Wexler's problems, meanwhile, seemed less severe. "I fell in love a hundred times in Jakarta," he said.

The end of the week's shooting brought photographers and project team to Bali's Nusa Dua Beach Hotel, for briefings and winding down. Director General Joop Ave announced to the press that the week's shoot had been a resounding success, thanks to good weather and cooperation by the people of Indonesia. "Now we can really celebrate" said co-publisher Owen, and everybody was invited to a final Farewell Party that night on the hotel's beachside grounds.

Shortly after twilight that evening, one of the biggest parties seen in Bali in recent years was opened. Director-General Ave welcomed all then announced with a grand gesture that it was time for the "show to begin". Perhaps a hundred *kecak* dancers emerged from behind nearby bushes bearing torches and chattering and chanting the sounds of this Balinese acapella opera. Following the fiery monkey dance, and the syncopation of a bamboo gamelan, 500-plus party guests and photographers proceeded to a big sit-down dinner in the open. Under the direction of Lueras, Hotel GM Paul Blake and Executive Chef Otto King an even bigger show began, featuring dueling *jegog* gamelan, *topeng* dancers from Batuan, Sundanese

minstrels, and state-of-the-art hip-hop music courtesy of Kuta Beach's Double Six Disco.

Guest of honor at the bash was Indonesia's Minister for Post, Telecommunications and Tourism, Bpk Soelilo Soedarman, and among the invited VIP guests were Christine Hakim, Indonesia's leading film star, and Ziggy Stardust himself, David Bowie. The Selamat Jalan party was hospitality at its best, Bali-style, and a fitting grand finale to the week – and the Voyage – that had ended the night before.

Early September, 1989 through August 1990

The project's shooting stars had finished taking their pictures, and the very next day Anne Greensall took all their gathered film with her on a flight to Sydney. Films were processed there, and then sent onwards to Millet's Paris office where he, his staff, designer Patrick Lebedeff and visiting photo editors began the massive task of editing the more than 120,000 photographs. Well-known author Edward Behr was commissioned to write the text, and during the coming months Helmi, Schoppert and Lueras also traveled to Paris to participate in the challenging photo editing process. With the advice and assistance of copublishers, Owen, Weldon and Ave, on visits to Paris, Millet's staff slowly began to pull all the rich material together. In Singapore meanwhile, the book's editor Schoppert coordinated all the editing and typesetting of text, and oversaw the book's color separation, printing and binding. After more than a year and a half of dealing with "the numbers" involved in producing this book, it is now finished *"sudah"* as they say in Indonesia – and it will serve for many years to come as a fitting commemoration of the 45th Anniversary of the Proclamation of the Independence of the Republic of Indonesia.

left to right: Indonesia's President Suharto meeting the Voyagers; Minister for Post, Telecommunications and Tourism Bpk Soelilo Soedarman welcomes publishers John Owen and Didier Millet; Creative Director Leonard Lueras and Public Relations coordinator Halida Ilahunde-Leclerc; Bpk Joop Ave, Publisher and Director General for Tourism; Meeting the press: John Owen, Didier Millet, Bpk Joop Ave and Halida Ilahunde-LeClerc; lunch at the Bogor Palace; *silat* experts show their skills; Halida Ilahunde-Leclerc and Didier Millet welcome Hilton GM Michael Schutzendorf; Bruno Barbey; Project Coordinator Ibu Seti-Arti Kailola; Raghu and Mihta Rai; at the welcome cocktail: Raghu Rai, G. A. Rossi, Ian Berry, Abbas, Richard Kalvar; Chief Photographer Rio Helmi with dancer; Launching the Voyage: Hilton Asst Manager Wolfgang Meier, Bpk Joop Ave, Alexander Millet, Project Director Dawn Low, John Owen, Didier Millet and Star Black; Project Editor Peter Schoppert; Mike Yamashita (he didn't resign); René Burri and Star Black; David Bowie and friend at the farewell party; Hiroshi Suga

from left to right, starting at top left: Minister for Post, Telecommunications and Tourism Bpk Soelilo Soedarman at the Bali farewell party; press conference at the Nusa Dua Beach Hotel; Pariwisata liaison man Tjetjep Suparman, Bpk Joop Ave and Didier Millet on board a Garuda flight over Java; photographers Basil Pao and Mark Wexler and little Paolet; Project Coordinator Amna S. Kusumo; Project Coordinator and photo editor Marie Claude Millet; Madam Soelilo Soedarman cutting the farewell cake; party entertainment from Pino Confessa; Magnum photographers Richard Kalvar, René Burri and Abbas on arrival; Dawn Low and Wolfgang Meier at the Bogor Palace; Bernard Hermann; Alexander Millet; the *kecak* dancers of Banjar Teges Kanginan, Peliatan, Bali; Guido Alberto Rossi and his assistant Gisella, Georg Gerster, and Mike Yamashita; Leonard Lueras and his daughter Asia; Mark Wexler and Paul Chesley enjoying Garuda; Ian Berry; and Didier Millet, Hanuman and friends gracing the farewell party that ended the Voyage through the Archipelago.

Abbas says he is "born a Third-worlder, now living in the West". Since 1970 Abbas has covered major political events in Africa, the Middle East, the Far East, Latin America and Europe. He has recently completed a one-year project photographing Mexico. A member of the Magnum Photo Agency, Abbas also recently won the first Olivier Rebbot Award.

Ping Amranand was born in Thailand in 1950, and now freelances in Washington DC specializing in editorial and corporate photography. His work has appeared in numerous leisure, travel and general interest publications such as *House and Garden*, *Architectural Digest* and *The Washington Post*. He has also held one-man shows in Thailand and the United States.

Bruno Barbey has been a member of the Magnum Photo Agency since 1966. Barbey has covered stories on every continent and his work is regularly featured in *Life*, *The Sunday Times*, *Stern*, *National Geographic*, *Geo* and *Paris-Match*. He has won many prestigious awards, and has exhibited his work in Paris, London, Rome and Zurich.

Back Tohir was born in 1951 in Palembang, South Sumatra. After studying photography and textiles in Cologne, Germany, he became a photographer, exhibiting and reporting throughout Europe. In 1980 he returned to Indonesia to join the government Mass Media and Documentation Secretariat. In 1982 he was named the official photographer for President Suharto on his visit to Europe, the US and the Far East, and since then he has traveled around the world covering important State occasions.

Ian Berry was born in Lancashire, England, and his prolific photographic career spans four decades. He has been a Magnum photographer since 1963, his work featuring in *The Sunday Times*, *Paris-Match* and *Life*. His photographs have been widely exhibited in London and Paris, including the first Photographic Exhibition at the Whitechapel Art Gallery, a joint Kodak Exhibition with McCullin, Snowdon, and Litchfield entitled "Britain in 1984". Recent works include coverage of the Cambodian refugees and an exhibition in Paris on South Africa. In 1988 he published *Black and White: l'Afrique du Sud par Ian Berry*.

Star Black turned to travel writing and photography while teaching English in Bangkok. In 1977 she joined United Press International as a staff news photographer and she now works as a freelance photographer based in New York. She has contributed to many newspapers and magazines including *The New York Times*, *Newsweek* and *The Washington Post*. Star co-authored the *Insight Guides* to Bali, Singapore and Malaysia, and her photographs appear in *A Day in the Life of Hawaii* and *Texas Boots*.

René Burri was born in 1933 in Zurich, and worked in film before beginning his association with Magnum in 1953. He became a full member of Magnum in 1959 and was instrumental in creating Magnum Films in 1965. Two years later he received the International Film and Television Award in New York. He was elected European Vice-President of Magnum in 1982 and inaugurated the Galerie Magnum in Paris with the exhibition "Terre de Guerre", co-curated with Bruno Barbey. A major retrospective of his work was presented in Zurich and Paris in 1984, and his work has been widely published in major books and exhibition catalogues.

Wendy Chan is a Singaporean freelance photographer specializing in editorial and travel stock photography. Represented by Image Bank, she has held several one-woman shows in Singapore. Her pictures can be seen in regional travel magazines such as Singapore Airlines' *Silver Kris*.

Paul Chesley — an American presently living in Aspen, Colorado — has been a freelance photographer working with National Geographic Society since 1975, travelling throughout Japan, Europe, South America and the United States. Solo exhibitions of his work have been held in the USA and Japan including a 1984 show at the Academy of Arts in Honolulu. His pictures can be seen in publications such as *Fortune*, *Geo*, *The Smithsonian* and *Esquire*.

Michael Freeman was born in St Annes, England in 1945. After studying at Oxford University and working in advertising in London, he began his photographic career in 1973. He is a frequent contributing photographer to *The Smithsonian* and his reportage work is widely published in *Geo*, *The Sunday Times Magazine* and *Paris-Match*. Following a Time-Life assignment in 1980-81 he has had a special interest in Southeast Asia and has published a number of books on the region including *Angkor: the Hidden Glories*.

Gerald Gay began his career practicing the craft of still-life photography. A partner of Developing Agents Photography, Singapore, since 1986, his pictures can be seen in Times Editions' *The New Art of Indonesian Cooking*, and *Cuisine Réunionnaise*, and in regional publications like *Signature* and *Interior Digest*.

Georg Gerster was born in Winterthur, Switzerland, and has travelled extensively in Europe, Africa, the Middle and Far East and the Americas. Gerster is a frequent contributor as a writer and photographer to *National Geographic*, *Paris-Match* and *Omni*. He has won major international awards and his books include *Grand Design* and *Over China*.

Ara Guler was born in Istanbul in 1928. He began

his career as a journalist and after meeting Marc Riboud and Cartier-Bresson began working on some assignments for Magnum Paris. In 1961 he was the first Turk to be elected to the American society of Magazine Photographers. He went on to be the correspondent in the East for *Life, Paris-Match* and *Stern*. He has photographed Winston Churchill, Picasso, the Shah of Iran, Salvador Dali and Auguste Renoir. In 1983 he completed the documentary film, *Death of a Hero*. Today he continues his reportage and portrait photography.

Desi Harahap was born in Jakarta in 1957, attended the Cinematography Academy in Jakarta (IKAJ) and has worked in feature and documentary film-making. She has since moved on to more journalistic work reporting on remote regions of Indonesia. She currently works as photo-editor of the weekly magazine *Jakarta-Jakarta*.

Rio Helmi was born in Indonesia in 1954. He has worked for ten years in the Indonesian media, as editor of the *Sunday Bali Post* from 1979-80, associate editor of *Mutiara* and contributor to *Tempo, Jakarta-Jakarta,* and various other magazines. He has also worked on film production and press promotions. His assignments have mainly been in Asia, his photographs appearing in various travel books on Bali and Indonesia, including the *Crafts of Indonesia, Bali High: Paradise from the Air,* and the forthcoming *Bali Style*. A partner in Image Network Indonesia, Rio acted as Chief Photographer and Assignment Editor for this book.

Bernard Hermann began his photography career working for major European newspapers and since then he has established himself as a full-time professional, travelling and working to produce titles on Guadeloupe, Haiti and Tahiti and its islands. He has also worked together with Les Editions du Pacifique on a series of pictorial albums about cities like San Francisco, Rio de Janeiro, New York, Paris, New Orleans, Sydney and London.

Mike Hosken is originally from Auckland New Zealand, and currently lives in New Caledonia. Hosken has been involved with photography and design work for almost nineteen years. His pictures relect his favorite pastimes — sailing, fishing, nature and the outdoors — and have appeared in publications like *Hi-Wind* and *Geo*. He is also the co-author of *New Caledonia: Ile de Lumieres* and *New Caledonia from the Air.*

Peter Hufgard was born in 1956 in Aschaffenburg, West Germany. He took up photography after school and travelled for two years round the world. He subsequently emigrated to New Zealand where he studied geology and geography at Otago University. He has travelled extensively in Asia and his photographic assignments have taken him as far afield as Antarctica. He has contributed articles and photographs to a number of newspapers and publications and has exhibited at the British Council, the Goethe Institute and New Zealand Embassy.

Richard Kalvar was born in 1944 and raised in Brooklyn, attended Cornell University and worked in New York City as an assistant to fashion photographer Jerome Ducrot. He then travelled throughout Europe until 1967. He returned to New York as a freelance photographer and in 1971 moved to Paris to join the photo agency VU. The following year he became a co-founder of the agency Viva. A full member of Magnum since 1977, he served as European Vice President from 1984 to 1988.

Kartono Riyadi was born in Pekalongan, Java, and is an experienced photojournalist and sports photographer. He is currently Photo Editor at the prestigious Kompas daily. His photographs have many awards, including certificates in the World Press Photo of the Year competition.

Martin Kers was born in Ridderkerk, Holland and spent his formative years playing in the landscapes which continue to inspire him. He studied fine arts at the Academy of Rotterdam, began work as an illustrator and turned to photography full time eight years ago. His work has appeared in *National Geographic* and *The Sunday Times*. He has won several national and international prizes including the International Kodak Prize in 1986.

Koes was born, raised and presently works on the island of Bali. He began freelance photography more than fourteen years ago. His strong interest in travel and advertising photography has taken him all over Asia, Europe and Australia. Koes is also the 1977 winner of two gold medal awards from the Indonesian Photographic Society (Federasi Photography Seluruh Indonesia).

Agus Leonardus became in 1970 a member of HISFA photo agency in Yogyakarta, of which he is now Secretary. In 1985 he founded the Indonesia Slide Club and organized three international slide exhibitions. His work has been widely exhibited and has won several awards internationally. His photographs have been published in books like *Flowers of Indonesia, Yogyakarta in Pictures* and *The Days of Sultan HB IX.*

Born in Hong Kong in 1946, **Leong Ka Tai** focuses mainly on editorial and corporate photography. He returned to Hong Kong in 1976 after working in Paris and founded his own studio there, Camera 22. His pictures have been published in international magazines including *Der Stern,* and in various books, including *China The Long March, Salute to Singapore, Beijing* and *The Taste of China.*

Leo Meier has been a specialist in wildlife and wilderness photography since migrating to Australia from Switzerland in 1971. Meier's work has been used in many conservation causes in Australia. Among many publications, his photographs have most recently been featured in *Australia The Beautiful Wilderness*, *Australia in Colour* and *Texas Wildflowers*. He also contributes to *National Geographic*

Robin Moyer is an accomplished photojournalist whose coverage of the conflict in Lebanon was recognized with two prestigious awards in 1983: the Press Photo of the Year Award in the World Press Photo competition and the Robert Capa Gold Medal Citation from the Overseas Press Club of America. A *Time* contract photographer based in Hong Kong and Tokyo, he is associated with Gamma-Liaison.

Kal Muller, born in Budapest, is a citizen of the USA. He has been travelling in Indonesia since 1970 and his work has been published in *National Geographic* and *Geo*. He is the author of a guidebook on Mexico, where he currently lives, and in 1987 his book *Indonesia: Paradise on the Equator* was published by Times Editions in Singapore.

Gueorgui Pinkhassov, born in Moscow, became interested in photography at school. Until 1978 he worked as an assistant in the Mossfilm studios. He then worked independently in Moscow as a photojournalist for a number of magazines. His work has been published in a variety of books and he has exhibited, individually and collectively, in Moscow and Paris, where he moved in 1985. In 1988 he became a member of the Magnum Photo Agency.

Basil Pao was born in Hong Kong, and later graduated from the Art Center College of Design, Los Angeles. His extensive career started in New York in 1973 and he has since worked in Hong Kong, Los Angeles, and New York as a designer, art director, writer and producer. In 1983, Basil was Art Director for the Macau sequence of *Indiana Jones and the Temple of Doom* and in August 1986 he joined Bertolucci's *The Last Emperor* crew in Beijing as Assistant Director, starring in the film as Prince Chun. Basil's photographs have featured widely in American and Asian magazines. He currently lives on Cheung Chan island.

Eddy Posthuma de Boer studied photography in The Hague, Holland. He began working as a newspaper photojournalist, and after covering the student revolts in Paris in the sixties, he turned to magazine assignments. His travel photography is featured in the glossy Dutch monthly *Avenue* and he is a staff photographer for the inflight magazines of KLM and Sabena.

Andre Pribadi has combined his longtime interests in photography and marine biology. His photographs documenting Indonesia's spectacular underwater heritage have appeared in publications all over the world. Currently he is working in Irian Jaya developing a new tourist center based around the recently discovered frontier diving grounds in the Cendrawasih Bay region.

Raghu Rai began working as a photographer in 1966 and since then he has been a regular contributor to *Time*, *National Geographic*, and *Paris-Match*. He was invited to join the Magnum Photo Agency in 1976 and has been a picture editor of *India Today* since 1980. He has twenty-five of his photographs in the permanent collection of the Bibliothèque Nationale in Paris. He has published several photography books including *Delhi: A Portrait*, *Indira Gandhi*, *The Taj Mahal*, *Calcutta*, and *Dreams of India*.

Guido Alberto Rossi was born in Milan in 1949. Rossi has long been a keen photo-journalist. He covered the Middle East and Indochina until 1973. Now focussing on sports and travel, Rossi is a qualified pilot and photographed *Florence from the Air* and *Tuscany from the Air*

Dominic Sansoni was selected by the Arts Council of Great Britain to participate in "The New British Image", an exhibition by young photographers in 1976. Now based in Sri Lanka his pictures can be seen in *Time* and *Asiaweek* and in several inflight magazines. He has photographed a guide to Kathmandu as well as *Sri Lanka: the Resplendent Isle*.

Santoso Alimin — born in Madiun in East Java in 1936 — learnt the art of photography at the age of eight from his father. He became a professional photographer in 1975 and has won various awards internationally since then. In the International Exhibition of Photography he was included as one of the top ten photographers from 1977 to 1982. In September 1983 he was appointed as a member of the jury of the Asian Salon in Singapore. He is also one of the founders of the Photography Institution of Surabaya.

Mahendra Sinh graduated with a Master's degree in Science and took up photography as a career fifteen years ago. His work has been exhibited in group shows in London and Chandigarh, India, and he staged an exhibition in the Soho Gallery in New York on "Afghanistan — A Will to Survive". Bombay-based Sinh's work has appeared in *The New York Times Magazine*, *Paris-Match* and

Newsweek and he is currently working on a book entitled *The Great Indian Desert.*

Fendi Siregar was born in Madiun, East Java, and his interest in photography began in school and continued through his studies in Communication Science at the Padjadjaran University. His accomplishments include The Architecture Photograpohy Award and the ICCU prize for World Children's Day. He has worked as a photo-editor with various publications, and with *Eksekutif* since 1979.

Tara Sosrowardojo was born in New York in 1952, and now lives in Jakarta. Although he majored in psychology and graphic design in Australia, photography was his minor subject and later became his career. His early professional photographs were stills for feature films. He currently produces audio-visual programs for industry and tourism, as well as working on commercial and editorial assignments. In 1980 he and partners formed the Zoom Photographic Agency.

Hiroshi Suga's photographs have appeared in many international publications. Winner of the 1987 Ken Domon Award, his various books on Bali, including *Bali Entranced* and *Bali: the Demonic, the Godly and the Wondrous* have received international acclaim. He has also held one-man shows in Japan and the United States.

Luca Invernizzi Tettoni is a proficient aerial, travel and commercial photographer and was one of the winners of the 1985 PATA Professionalism Award for specific contributions to the promotion of Southeast Asia. A photograph from his internationally acclaimed *Thai Style* recently appeared on the cover of *Architectural Digest.* He has photographed for many other fine arts and travel books such as *Ten Contemporary Thai Artists*, and *Thailand a View from Above.*

Andreas Darwis Triadi was born in Solo in October 1954 and began his career in photography in 1980. His accomplishment is both nationally and interntionally acknowled-

ged. In 1982 he received the Gold medal in the Calendar category of the "National Gobel" Matsusita Award. He has participated in several courses in photography in Switzerland, Germany, England and Singapore. Darwis held solo and joint exhibitions from 1982 to 1986. He is also Chairman of APPI (The Indonesian Association of Professional Photographers) and the Jakarta Photographers Society.

Peter van der Velde supported his early interest in photography as a KLM steward. In 1968 his break came when he was recruited to assist the famous Dutch photographer Kees Scherer on assignment for the Dutch women's magazine, *Magriet.* He turned freelance in 1972 and contributes to *Avenue, Panorama,* and American Express magazines. He published a six volume series on French and Spanish wines, and *The Great Wines of Bordeaux and Burgundy.* Peter travels and shoots extensively around the world.

Steve Vidler was born in Dover, England, and has been a photojournalist specializing in travel for twenty-two years. With bases in Tokyo and London, he travels the world, and his photos have been published in many magazines. He has publi-

shed *Asia in Focus*, and has contributed to books on countries like Switzerland, Singapore, and Peru.

Mark Wexler first took up a camera as a research tool during fieldwork for anthropologist Gregory Bateson. He then turned to magazine photography and his work has appeared in *Time, Life,* and *National Geographic.* He received three World Press Awards for his work on *A Day in the Life of Japan.* Mark lives in New York and is a member of the American Society of Magazine Photographers .

Mike Yamashita was born in San Francisco, raised in New Jersey and spent six years living in Asia after graduating from Wesleyan University. He is regular contributor to *National Geographic* and works for corporate clients such as Nikon, Singapore Airlines and Diners Club on worldwide assignments. His book, *Lakes, Peaks and Prairies: Discovering the US-Candian Border* was published in 1984.

The Authors
Gavin Young studied modern history at Oxford, and after travels in the Middle East –

which later formed the basis of his acclaimed *Return to the Marshes* – he joined the *Observer* as a foreign correspondent. In 1980, he set off on a long series of voyages by sea, journeys described in *Slow Boats to China* and *Slow Boats Home.* He has returned often to Indonesia, traveling by sea, in the tracks of Joseph Conrad and other great travelers of the last century.

Edward Behr was brought up in France and Britain, and first came to Indonesia as a young officer in the Indian Army. He served in Padang, Sumatra and later in India during Partition. After graduating from Cambridge University, he joined Reuters as a correspondent, later covering Indonesia in the 1960s while heading the *Newsweek* Hong Kong bureau. Behr has written several books, including *Anyone Here Been Raped and Speaks English?*, on his experiences as a foreign correspondent, and *The Last Emporer,* the biography of Pu Yi, as well as an acclaimed biography of Emperor Hirohito of Japan.

Paul Zach has been writing about Indonesia for more than ten years. He worked there as a correspondent for a variety of publications including *Newsweek.* He is the author of *Indonesia: Paradise on the Equator,* and *Indonesia: Images from the Past.*

Garuda Indonesia

Established in 1949, Garuda is the flagship and parent company of a major group involved in air transport and related industries. Garuda Indonesia — which is considered the largest airline in the Southern Hemisphere — operates to 35 domestic centers and 30 international cities on five continents. Equipped with high standard maintenance facilities, the largest hangar in Asia and a modern training center, Garuda Indonesia is building its position as an internationally recognized airline.

Pertamina, the State Oil and Gas Company, manages the country's oil and gas industry, and its activities cover exploration, production, refining, supply and distribution throughout the country as well as internationally. Pertamina possesses two LNG plants with a total production of 22.1 million metric tons per year, which ranks Indonesia as the largest LNG producer in the world. In the petrochemical field Pertamina produces methanol, polyprophelene, and paraxylene.

Eastman Kodak Company's Professional Photography Division (PPD) designs, develops, and manufactures products to meet the needs of professional photographers worldwide. These include color transparency and negative films, black and white films, papers, display products, and chemistry. Under the leadership of Raymond H DeMoulin, PPD has become increasingly active in sponsoring workshops, exhibits, and books … all of which are aimed at developing and recognizing high quality professional photography.

The Hilton has 644 well-appointed guest-rooms, suites, a Presidential suite, and a penthouse suite and 256 fully-serviced residential apartments at the Hilton towers. This 32 acre complex includes 14 restaurants and bars, ranging from exquisite dining to casual outdoor snacks, and extensive sport and recreational facilities. Catering to an international clientele, its five star diamond rating ensures superior professional service at international standards, offering gracious Indonesian hospitality.

A deluxe beach front resort that blends superb modern comfort and traditional Balinese architecture, the Nusa Dua Beach Hotel was inaugurated by President Suharto of Indonesia on 28 May 1983. The hotel is idyllically located on the southern peninsula of Bali about 10 minutes from the International Airport. It is a perfect example of the outstanding artistry that can be found on Bali, a five star diamond hotel and paradise as well.

In 1968 a government-owned company bought the shares of PT Asuransi Timur Jauh (established as a private company in 1953); since then the company has become the sister company of PT PP Berdikari. The company since 1972 has conducted extensive changes in policies and now pursues an aggressive development program in an effort to achieve potential growth, dynamic progress and new levels of professionalism.

BANK CENTRAL ASIA

BCA — established in 1957 — emerged as the leading domestic private national bank in terms of assets and profitability. In 1989 its total assets reached US$ 2,500 million and over 8500 people were employed in 200 domestic and five international offices; BCA also became the first bank in Southeast Asia to be authorized to issue Visa's Travelers Checks. Introduced in 1980, BCA Card was the first credit card denominated in Rupiahs.

Bank Dagang Negara — a state-owned commercial bank — was founded on April 11, 1960. It is the fourth largest bank in Indonesia, with a domestic network of 153 branch offices, agencies in New York and Los Angeles, representative offices in Singapore and Hong Kong, and hundreds of correspondent banks worldwide. Bank Dagang Negara can assist the development of your business and is always ready to satisfy ever-growing public demand for the banking services.

BANK INTERNASIONAL INDONESIA

BII is a leading member of the BII Group of 16 financial institutions which, with two other groups, constitute the large Sinar Mas Group comprising all together 73 companies owned by the prominent Indonesian entrepreneur Eka Tjipta Wijaya. With expanding assets which have grown 58-fold in seven years, BII plans to set up an average number of 20 branch offices each year.

On July 5, 1946, Bank Negara Indonesia 1946, widely known as Bank BNI was the first state-owned bank founded after Indonesia's Independence. Bank BNI operates throughout Indonesia as well as in major international money markets with 284 domestic branches, six foreign branches and hundreds of correspondent banks globally. Currently Bank BNI is the biggest bank in Indonesia. Activities of Bank BNI include traditional and non-traditional banking.

Bank Umum Nasional — a private foreign exchange bank — was established in 1952. The bank actively pursues all kinds of traditional and modern banking activities. It has a large network operating in the main business centers in Indonesia and has corresponding connections with well-known banks on five continents. With experienced professionals, supported by up-to-date technology the bank could become a partner for your business, surely leading you to success.

BAKRIE
GROUP OF COMPANIES

The Bakrie business was established in 1942 as Bakri and Brothers Commodity Trading and Commission Agent. Later it became Indonesia's pioneer in steel pipe manufacturing. Diversification in the 80s has made Bakrie a group of companies with more than 40 subsidiaries and affiliated companies with activities in manufacturing, agriculture, mining, financial services, property management, leisure, contracting and trading industries.

Plaza INDONESIA
SHOPPING CENTER

PT Bimantara Eka Santosa was established in 1983. The core businesses are trading and development of hotels and office and retail space. This company is the developer of Jakarta's Plaza Indonesia, the largest premier shopping center in Southeast Asia, comprising 40,000 sq meters of floor area, and the adjoining Grand Hyatt Hotel of 455 all-suite rooms.

PT Bogasari Flour Mills — established in 1969 was born to serve the world's largest archipelago, Indonesia. With mills in Jakarta and Surabaya, Bogasari has one of the biggest milling operations in the world. These two complexes are equipped with the latest facilities, supporting production which reaches some 5000 tons per day. A workforce of around 2000 people is managed by Sudwikatmono (Director) and Soedono Salim (Chairman) from its Head Office in Wisma Indocement.

Started as a trading concern in Surabaya 36 years ago, Dharmala Group now consists of over 100 companies. Its scope of business includes trading, manufacturing, plantation operation, real estate development and construction, financial services, heavy equipment distribution, consumer services and tourism related activities. Dharmala Group, with its head office in Jakarta, operates in other major cities of Indonesia and

Singapore, Hong Kong, Philippines, Thailand, the United States and the UK.

"Imagine a land where anything is possible" is the slogan of Indobuildco, founded in 1971, focusing on the building construction business. The Jakarta Hilton International Hotel and Executive Club were the first projects completed in 1976. "Lanais" and "Bazaar" followed in 1979, the Garden Tower Wing in 1984. Hilton High Rise Residences I and II, completed in 1989, provide comfort and security to expatriates who come to stay in Jakarta.

Kayumas / Diamond Furniture started with its roots in the logging industry more than two decades ago in forest-rich Kalimantan. From its humble beginnings the Company has grown into a diversified conglomerate with business interests in logging, plywood, blackboard, paper overlaid plywood, saw-milling, moulding products, ceramic tiles, wooden and rattan furniture, etc. Kayumas recently established Diamond Furniture, a manufacturer of knock-down home and office furniture with marketing capabilities in Asia, Europe and the United States.

KLM — founded on October 7, 1919 — is the oldest airline in the world. As a pioneer in civil aviation KLM has consistently developed its modern passenger services. KLM's reputation for reliability and quality regularly ranks it among the leading international airlines of the world. In 1924 KLM operated the world's first intercontinental flight to Indonesia. Now, more than 50 years later KLM serves 144 destinations in 77 countries. KLM's special relationship with Indonesia, however, continues.

PT MANTRUST

PT Mantrust – the acronym for Management Trust Company – was established on January 20, 1958, and began producing candies and biscuits. Over the past 30 years, from modest beginnings Mantrust has been able to broaden its horizons by expansion in addition to establishing a wide reputation as a major agro-industries company. It is a major leader in both Indonesia's agro-industries and canned food industry, as well as in its other newer business ventures.

In the late 60s Rayan Wijaya, chairman of the Rayan Group went about the business of establishing a group of companies that

now, one way or another, participate in all facets of Indonesia's ever expanding industry — *Advertising and Marketing, Aviation Engineering, Corporate Design, Food and Beverage, Gas and Petroleum, Gifts and Souvenirs, Hotels and Tourism, Interior Architecture, Manufacturing, and Public Relations.*

Sang Pelopor – the Pioneers – groups five leading real estate developers in Indonesia: Jaya Group, Metropolitan Development Group, Pondok Indah Group, Bumi Serpong Damai and Citra Habitat Group. Each of them has won a high reputation for professionalism as experienced real estate developers in Jakarta and other cities. They are known for their pioneering spirit in building satellite towns and Indonesia's first self-contained city.

Drs Siddharta & Siddharta, established in 1957, was one of the first registered public accountancy firms in Indonesia. In 1987 we united our local experience with international expertise to create one of the country's largest practices. Today, Drs Siddharta & Siddharta in association with Coopers & Lybrand provide a comprehensive range of financial advice to businesses in the private and public sectors.

Bank Dagang Negara Indonesia was established in 1945 as Indonesia's first foreign exchange bank. The only National Private Bank, BDNI has grown throughout the years as Indonesia develops.

Bank Bumi Daya is a state-owned bank, with branches in Indonesia and around the world. At the end of March 1990 the bank had 176 domestic branches, four subsidiaries, and representative offices or branches in Singapore, Hong Kong, London, Tokyo, New York, and the Cayman Islands.

In the short time since its founding, Humpuss Group Indonesia, a conglomerate of Humpuss-owned companies, has become one of Indonesia's most reliable business groups. The group's activities extend into the fields of trade and services as well as into industry and manufacturing. Its youthful and professional management gives the group the vision and the dynamism necessary to create a better future for itself and its clients.

The Rajawali Group is a diversified conglomerate with a wide range of businesses throughout Indonesia.

ACKNOWLEDGEMENTS

A project of this size and complexity would have been impossible without the generous assistance of many people. We have tried to name as many of those people as we can. In addition, we would like to thank all those who assisted the photographers in the field. A special word of thanks is reserved for those people who assisted by consenting to be photographed. This group of Voyagers remembers fondly the times you shared with us. And we are sure that this book's readers will as well.

for their generous additional sponsorship

Great River Garments
Gatari Helicopters,
especially Capt Paul
Unilever Indonesia,
for sponsoring the batik shirts

at the Directorate-General of Tourism

Burhan
Dusep
Rusdi
Yati
Risna
Mursanto
Mahmudin

at Garuda Indonesia Airlines

Mr Soeparno PDG, President Director
Mr Susikto, VP (Commercial)
Mr M Kamdhi, Director of Marketing
Moestafa Haidar
Ibu Joke Rayanto
Ibu S Rosina Harijadi
Ibu Suci
Ibu Emmy Dasuki

at the Jakarta Hilton International

Michael Schuetzendorf
Rudy Saleh
Wolfgang Maier
Rudi and the Hilton Art Department
Ibu Pepin and Ibu Irma
from the Hilton Business Center
the Food and Beverage Department

at Eastman Kodak

Robert Williamson
Stephen Lee
Jeff McLeod

at Setia Tours

Nurdin Purnomo
Ernie A.L. Setiawan
Lily Setiawan

in Jakarta

Lucky Dirgantara
Pauline Goh
Jozeph Grounewoud
Daryono
and the staff of the Istana Bogor
Presidential Palace
Didier Hammel
Brian van den Hurk
Lisnawati
Irsan Lubis
Setiawati Lubis
Gilles Leclerc
Sampurno
of the Presidential Household
Maureen Santoso
Lin Soegiarto
Herman Suhermanto
Suwati Kartiwa
The Armed Forces
of the Republic of Indonesia
The Duta Art Gallery
The Asmat Foundation

in Bali

Pino Confessa
Made Badung
Amde Djimat
Andy Toth
Brent Hesselyn
Albert Beaucourt
Igor Musik
Marco Cecere
Ida Ayu Pujastuti
Surya Djelantik
I Made Budi
Wana Mahogany
Nyoman Djayus
Top Star Beauty Salon
the *kecak* dancers of Banjar Teges
Kanginan, Peliatan
Double Six disco, Kuta Beach
Kora Amalwati
I Gusti Nyoman Ngurah Widnyana

at the Nusa Dua Beach Hotel, Bali

Paul Blake
Stanley Allison
Otto King
Beta Ganjar

in Jogjakarta

F.X.A. Samsoel Hadi
Charlie Kushner
Yamin Makawaru
Ledjar Subroto
Bruce Granquist

in Irian Jaya

Sam Chandra
David Wunsch

in Paris

Marie Amelie Berri
Jacques Dumarçay
François Hebel
Kunang Helmi
Michel Picard
Camilla Sandell
Dominique Thomas

in Singapore

Idayu and Mastura
Campos-Chan Chiu Leng
Chee Wai Ping
Clifford Gan
Kok Weng Chin
Lee Chor Lin
Loo Say San
Gina Mok and Eric Koh
Lawrence Nonis
Tuti Sunario
Eileen Thong
Freddy Wong
Woon Mee Lan

in Sydney

Kumar Pereira
Andrew Nairn
Graham Richardson
Beverley Sharpe
Shirley Soh
Ron Tobiasz

Elsewhere

John Falconer and Greta Weil in London
Tony Greensall in Hong Kong

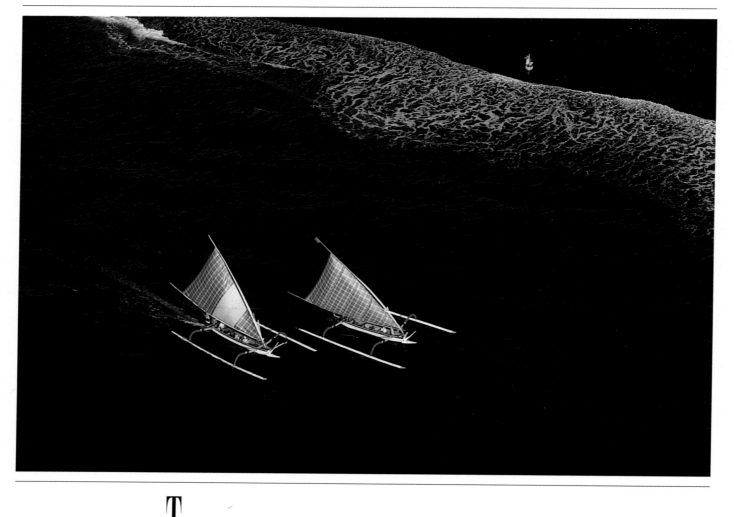

The triangular sails of traditional Balinese fishing boats skim across the ocean like huge insects searching for food from the sea. Even though the Balinese are an island people they do not venture beneath the waves too often—they believe that the sea is a place for the spirits of the underworld. Like their boats, they are content to skim.

Third Edition Printed in Singapore in 1997.